My HEART Rejoices

ONE BENEDICTINE SISTER'S SPIRITUAL AUTOBIOGRAPHY

MARY McGEHEE, O.S.B.

Published by
Canticle Press
916 Convent Road NE
Cullman AL 35055-2019
U. S. A.
smmcgehee@gmail.com

Cover design by: Sarah Dockery - Sudoc Designs
www.sudocdesigns.com

Original Cover photograph by Bradley Mason
www.istockphoto.com

ISBN0-9786401-0-1

Printed in the United States of America

My heart proclaims the greatness of the Lord.
My spirit takes delight in God, my Savior,
who has looked upon this lowly servant.

Luke 1:46-48

Contents

Introduction: Who Do You Say I Am? vi

Chapter 1: Earliest Memory 1

Chapter 2: The Heart of Christ 5

Chapter 3: How Did I Know God? 9

Chapter 4: The God of the Stranger 14

Chapter 5: Bride of Christ 19

Chapter 6: Miss Perfect 25

Chapter 7: The Gropers 31

Chapter 8: Darkness 43

Chapter 9: Refugees 53

Chapter 10: Justice 66

Chapter 11: Year of Jubilee 77

Chapter 12: Body and Soul 83

Chapter 13: Centering 91

Chapter 14: My Brother John 96

Chapter 15: Passage through Death 104

Chapter 16: Put Away your Sword 114

Chapter 17: My Heart Rejoices 120

Acknowledgements 122

Introduction: WHO DO YOU SAY I AM?

What are the names I call my Beloved? This has been a long love story, a lifetime of being drawn and enticed and wooed and loved. For the most part I stay busy with one thing or another: productive work, interesting engagements, meaningful ministry. But now and then my attention is drawn. I am caught or turned or dropped or moved in a way to open the eyes of my soul, and I am given a glimpse. For my lover is the Divine One who has ever held me and won't leave me alone.

A few summers ago I was given a life review, almost a near-death experience in which a lifetime passed in an instant before my eyes. Oh, I was not anywhere near death, so I thought at that time. Rather, I was enjoying a mountaintop week of retreat at St. Mary's Retreat Center in Sewanee, Tennessee, where my lifetime of these glimpses passed before my eyes within a single moment.

It happened this way: David Frenette, our retreat director, led a guided meditation, something I had done many times before. I was readily settling into it. After guiding us through some relaxation and steps to our interior space, we were invited to meet Jesus with the crowd that always pressed around him. I experienced Jesus looking at me as David asked, "Who do you say I am?" I was delighted to be there. I was ready for this question, anticipating a new knowing dropping down from the heavens or surfacing from my unconscious. "Show me yourself," I cried within. Instead I saw a stream of scenes I already knew so well. They were my experiences of God, my God moments, during the past sixty years. At first I stomped my foot because I wanted more. I wanted something new, something deeper and more profound. But there was only silence in that direction.

So I found myself going to my room to journal what I had been shown. As I did I was gifted with a great tenderness and awe.

God has been so patient with me for so long, ever drawing me, ever creating me.

I knew I had to write in order to claim this love at deeper levels within myself. I also felt I was meant to share this ordinary story with others. Perhaps my story can help others own their personal stories and thereby claim even more strongly the ever-drawing love of our Beloved. Much of this spiritual autobiography is so simple, but it is my story humbly offered. It offers my strong moments of deep knowing.

I remember at a prayer gathering one night over a decade ago a beautiful man smiled at my sister companion and me as he asked us to share our mystical experiences. Margaret Mary and I looked at one another and shrugged. The life of a sister is so simple. There is seldom high drama, even in the inner life. Ours is a life of dailyness, rhythmed with scripture and liturgy that could lull one to sleep, or it could be the wave to keep one focused on the Ultimate.

So I offer you the remembrances I was gifted with that summer day. Perhaps they will encourage you to notice the God-threads in your own ordinary life. At the end of each section there is a suggestion for personal reflection. Though each chapter is short, I suggest you read only one chapter at a sitting so you can spend time with your own story if you are so inclined.

My
HEART
Rejoices

Chapter 1: EARLIEST MEMORY

I was born in St. Louis, Missouri. My first two and a half years we lived on Newport Avenue in Webster Groves. My family members at that time were Daddy, Mother, John and me. John, who was three years older than me, was mildly brain-damaged at birth, though I did not know that for many years. He and I did everything together as children. I am told that at age two I was already acting responsibly for him. One day when mean kids up the street pushed him down and took his hat, I marched up there and got his hat back. But that happened before I can remember.

My first memory involved our family move across St. Louis from Webster Groves to Yale Avenue in Richmond Heights. I can still feel myself standing in our old house, the only one I had ever known. It was totally empty, no furniture or belongings left, just bare wooden floors and plain walls with no pictures or other decoration. The house echoed with our footsteps. I was uneasy and insecure at leaving all I had ever known. I felt fear and loss. I stood in the middle of a seemingly very large room with Mother beside me and asked her, "Did we get our galoshes?" I think I had just gotten my first pair of rain shoes. The feeling I remember was one of anxiety and great responsibility. At age two and a half I already felt responsible for important things. Mother's response was, "Yes, we have the galoshes. Don't worry." And I felt a wave of great relief sweep over me, now comforted and secure. All the really important things would be taken care of. I could let go and trust, feeling the maternal care and warmth of her reassurance.

******

It was theologian Jim Bacik from Bowling Green State University who gave the Benedictine Sisters a workshop in the mid-1970s, and so helped me get in touch with this earliest memory. He called it one's "primary intuition," and suggested we recall it in as

1

much detail as possible—all the negative and all the positive aspects of it, and all the accompanying emotions. Jim told us that this scene, as primary intuition, can often point to our understanding of God. These feelings continue to connect to how we envision and relate to God throughout our lives.

I could have been Abraham called out of the land I knew as home. Even at two and a half I felt responsible for the welfare of the tribe: "Did we get our galoshes?" Throughout life I know I have carried this same felt responsibility for the group, in the ministries in which I have served or for many years now for my Benedictine Sisters. My dreams often echo this. But with the responsibility is anxiety and fear. Will we make it? Is everything taken care of?

Again and again I hear Mother God say, "Yes, we have everything that is needed. Do not be afraid. Do not worry. Come on. Let's move." Each time that I catch myself worrying, I laugh that I have once again been caught worrying about our galoshes. And I am always wondrously released and comforted by the secure foundation of my life, my God who is Mother and Father and constant provider. I laugh at myself for worrying about our galoshes once again.

Over and over in life I have to admit an illusion I live with— that I can control my destiny, that I can make things better, that I can even make myself better or holier or more perfect. Oh yes, one does have to take responsibility for life, but I more often err in the imbalance of thinking I am in charge. Each time that I wake up to my illusion, I am once again surprised by the graciousness of life and the Giver of all life. All is truly taken care of and in extraordinarily beautiful ways. I have only to open my eyes and see.

REFLECTION

Maybe you can take a breath and think back:
What is your earliest memory? It does not
matter what age you were. Whatever is the
earliest memory is significant in itself.
Who was there? What happened?
What are all the details? What feelings did you have?

Spend time in the archeological dig of memory, fleshing out the scene and the feelings as fully as possible. Perhaps you can trace this set of feelings and reactions throughout your life. Perhaps it can give a clue about your relationship with God.

I remember an evening about twenty years ago with both of my parents and a few of our Sisters. We each pondered and shared our earliest memories together. It was a beautiful sharing, a wonderful bonding experience. Maybe there are others you trust enough with whom you would like to do this kind of sharing.

3

Jim Bacik's instructions are the following:

1. Reflect on your primary negative intuition: for example, an abiding sense of unworthiness; the absurdity of suffering; the inability to find an imperishable love; the fragmentation of the world and human existence. Think of your first remembered experience as a clue. This comes from the psychologist Alfred Adler.

2. Think of your primary positive intuition: life makes sense despite absurdity; we will find an enduring love; there is a unifying force more powerful than fragmentation.

3. Think of a Bible story which reflects this primary intuition.

4. Compose a prayer around the experience.
   (Letter from Jim Bacik, August 2004)

4

Chapter 2: THE HEART OF CHRIST

I have a wonder-full prayer that has been with me most of my life. It was given to me at age five. I know my parents taught me my first prayers, the "Our Father" and the "Hail Mary," the prayer before meals, and "Now I Lay Me Down to Sleep" before bed. But my first formal theology was taught in kindergarten.

I went to kindergarten at Little Flower Catholic School in St. Louis and had a wonderful Dominican Sister who deeply loved God, and just as deeply desired to share this love with her little charges. She taught us how much God loved us, and she taught us to offer ourselves to God every morning. She said if we did this in the morning our whole day would be God-centered. I joyfully wanted this. As a small child I had a very strong sense of God's presence and love. Sister said we could pray a long prayer of morning offering—offering every thought, every word, every deed, every action to God. Or we could very simply pray, "All for Thee, O Most Sacred Heart of Jesus." That this one line would summarize all our desire deeply impressed me. I prayed this little prayer fervently, and I knew what I was praying. I truly meant every word, and I had a strong sense of the presence of God as I prayed it. I still do. I wanted to give God every thought, every word, every deed and every action—my whole being. The prayer embodied my full desire to give all to the One I knew loved me and had given all to me: "All for Thee, O Most Sacred Heart of Jesus."

Later when I learned Centering Prayer in my forties, we were cautioned not to use our "sacred word" outside of our specific centering prayer period. The "sacred word" is a single word that one uses to quiet into a state of deep meditation and stillness. During our work-a-day world, we were told we could pick an "active prayer phrase" or sentence, something that could continue to remind us of God's presence throughout the rest of the day. This phrase could be used any time our mind was free and our desire was to remember the strong presence of God—while in checkout lines in the grocery store, waiting for a stoplight to change, while in a traffic jam, paused with canned music during a phone call. I realized I already had such a sentence, that it had resided within me and that I had used it frequently since age five.

Most often I use it in the way I was taught—to give every aspect of my day to God, to offer my heart that it may be bonded to the Heart of God. Even though I may not keep my attention constantly turned in unceasing prayer, I daily make my intention with this simple, deep and heart-felt way. God who is ever gracious, takes my intention most seriously and flowers it.

Sometimes in infrequent moments of profound prayer I simply sit with the Heart of Christ, marveling at His total poured-out-ness, this heart love of God, this mystery of the All Holy One coming into flesh, taking on the full human condition unto death into life. I sit speechless in a heart-to-heart with the One who gave all. I pour out my own heart issues. I open my heart to receive. I linger in union.

Sometimes as I pray this prayer my desire is to pour myself out. Usually this sentiment comes as I experience compassion to someone in need who has appeared at my door—the spiritually thirsty more often than not. And I wish to give to the suffering Christ before me.

Sometimes I am totally distracted, and the phrase is an anchor to bring me back to the real world. Almost always when I pray this prayer, I have a visceral feeling of good energy within me, a feeling that since childhood has meant a God-connection. This small prayer has been a mainstay and a very dear companion. It is an anchor, a sustaining impulse to keep me in touch with my Center.

Sometimes as I pray this little prayer I hear the Beloved speak to me: "All for thee, Mary." I touch God's passion to gift me with life and beauty, flower and birdsong and all the wonders that come with the rhythms of sunshine and moonlight and the seasons of the year. I drink in the thoughtfulness and creative ecstasy of my Beloved.

Many years passed before one day I realized that in my desire to give my all to the heart of God, I had been brought into that very heart. I have lived since age seventeen at Sacred Heart Monastery, surrounded by images and experiences of love and caring, living in the daily heartbeat of the monastic prayer rhythms that keep me focused on the Gracious One.

It has taken me a long time to realize the deceptive simplicity of this prayer. It focuses and anchors my will toward Love. On my dullest and most boring day, I pray this prayer to remind me of my entire reason for being. In my times of greatest elation, I pray in praise and to direct my heart to its Source. In frustration and anger it cools me. In sorrow with life's bitterness I remember the Gracious One who holds me still. It is like a dart through the blinding overgrowth of life's lostness, loneliness, hurriedness and frenetic pace. When life shifts and changes, as it hopefully will so I may constantly grow and develop, this prayer roots me to the one thing that truly matters, to the One who is my Source, to my God.

REFLECTION

Do you have such an active prayer phrase that has been with you for years? Perhaps a meaningful scripture or a line from a favorite hymn? If not from the archeology of your early life, you can still make a selection. Choose seven to twelve syllables.

This active prayer phrase can also be composed by pondering two things:

—the name of God or the quality of God currently most meaningful to me

—the greatest need I have presently in my spiritual life

Then make a cry for help using five to twelve syllables stating these two things.

Do you have a small child in your life—a daughter or son, grandchild or dearly loved one? What simple and clear prayer resides deeply within you that you would like to share with this little person? Think carefully. What prayer would you most like to teach this small child, a prayer that may have a lifetime impact?

Chapter 3: HOW DID I KNOW GOD?

All that I knew about God in my childhood came from my Catholic culture, which was the major context of my life growing up. As a small child in the 1940s I lived in St. Louis, a Catholic city of the triumphalistic church with massive, golden churches. It was a sensual and sensuous experience, appealing and gratifying.

I remember the bong of the great church bells, calling us within. And the deep, echoing silence inside the churches. It was a silence of Mystery and awe. It made one want to tiptoe, or for small children to test the echoes with a squeal or the call of a single syllable that could reverberate in the immense space. Yet it was totally comfortable with the snap of women's pocketbooks as they extracted their rosaries and jingled them in prayer. There was the familiar smell of wax on floors or the chill of marble, the wood of the kneelers knocking to let rows of people in or out, up or down. There was the fragrance of incense and Easter lilies, and the mystery of the tinkling bells at the moment of consecration when we all looked up to gaze at the white host breaded Body of Christ, then lower our heads in reverence and beat our breasts with "O Lord, I am not worthy." There were the statues of saints, the gold and candles and flowers bedecking the high altar. The priests in brightly colored vestments swished by chanting in Latin, the proud language that was used around the world and made us Catholic/Universal.

The Catholic culture enfolded me, especially the Catholic schools with the nuns in ancient garb enclosing the whole body except for their face and hands, women of strict discipline, love of learning, and total dedication to God. We children lined up for processions, hands folded, falling to one knee in unison with the head sister's clicker, boys in their altar server outfits, girls dropping flower petals before the Blessed Sacrament on Holy Thursday or carrying nosegays for Mary's altar in May. We had Benediction of the Blessed Sacrament and Forty-Hours Devotion in adoration of the Divine Presence in the brilliant gold monstrance, the mandala of wonder, chanting in Latin or awed in silence, processing inside and out with candles and incense.

At home we prayed together before each meal and knelt by the bed for our nightly prayers. In our neighborhood, we met regularly for the block rosary, gathering in a different house on our street each week, all on our knees except the ill or most elderly or my Presbyterian father. We listened religiously to Monsignor Fulton J. Sheen on TV with his hidden angel who erased his scholarly words from the blackboard. We saw movies with Catholic actors and actresses: Loretta Young, Margaret O'Brien, Grace Kelly, Bing Crosby, and Bob Hope.

We memorized the Baltimore catechism and knew everything (we thought) about our Catholic faith. I loved the Bible stories of high adventure, but have to admit I never picked up the Bible until I was in public high school in the South.

How could I not be overcome by the Mystery?!! I reveled in it all, proud and confident. I loved to make visits to the church on my own, awed in the silence. I lived each day with a strong sense of the presence of God. Thankfully, I experienced parents, teachers, and pastors who were exemplary, yet very ordinary.

I was a happy, active child, and that visceral feeling of childhood energy and play I relate to my sense of God, of Mystery, and of celebrating Life. I was the queen of the playground, organizing games, shouting, laughing, calling in great energy. I played hard, swinging by my knees from the trapeze and making flips off, landing on my feet. There was roller skating with skates that screwed to my oxfords, when I would start at the top of our big hill and speed down skipping all the cracks in the sidewalk. We played cops and robbers, or cowboys and Indians, and had snowball fights with snow in winter and with white ball flowers in the summer. John and I built a clubhouse on our sandbox after pulling our wagon to the

10

corner grocery to load it with old orange crates, then ripping the boards apart to nail them along the uprights fastened to the sandbox. We played dolls on rainy days, if I promised not to tell other kids that John and his friend David played dolls with me.

Both of my parents grew up on farms. I remember summers on Mother's family farm in Kansas, going to sleep with the wind whistling around the corners of the house. It felt so secure hearing that sound, as if the Living Presence were all around. I could totally relax in the old soft bed upstairs. Both of my parents were tied to the soil, always tending a garden. They were both college graduates and deeply loved science, spoke of it often, showing us the beauties of nature and its wondrous balance. We were all involved in scouting throughout childhood to enjoy the great wonders of nature. The mysteries of nature and science were always equated with the great Mystery of God.

I delighted in my childhood cultural experiences of faith, religion, family, and God. I give deep thanks for all these gifts from my parents and my faith community.

I cannot remember when I did not know God. I knew Him in the winter ice that made me late for school because I had to test it on every mud puddle. I sensed the Presence in the summer thunderstorms, and St. Louis had many sudden ones. I was totally enthralled by the power and beauty and majesty of a storm, sometimes sitting on the porch swing to be as close as I could in absorbed fascination. I knew God sitting with my family on the front porch on a summer evening, listening to the cicadas in the sycamores, traffic passing by, children's voices calling out down the street. Sometimes we could hear the lions roar or the sea lions call from the St. Louis Zoo nearby. We just listened and were, and were family. The Presence seemed to be with me always. I would talk to Him about my little difficulties and be overjoyed at each new act of creation, such as our new puppy.

What did I know about God? He was the One of Mystery and awe, but also the One who made me and loved everything about me, as my parents did. The One who wanted me to be good and loving, not to be a bad girl. He was more than Santa Claus, bigger, all encompassing, the One who was creator and sustainer and magical balancer of the Mystery that surrounded us.

I remember as a young adult being asked, "When did you come to know the Lord Jesus? When did you turn your life over to Jesus, accepting him as your personal Savior?" I was utterly puzzled by the question. I had never *not* known Him. My life was held by Him. I could not even fathom any other possibility.

REFLECTION
What was your childhood sense of the
Mystery of God?

Who helped support your belief?

How was this done?

Was there a culture or framework to help enhance the sense of
Mystery? Describe.

Express your gratitude for these gifts.

Chapter 4: THE GOD OF THE STRANGER

When I was nine everything changed in my Catholic world. In the early 1950s we moved to Tuscaloosa, Alabama, which was predominantly Protestant. The Catholic culture, the very place in which I had thrived, now divided me from others. As a Catholic I felt like an oddity, interrogated about my strange beliefs and watched every Friday to see if I would eat meat. All the neighbor kids were Protestants and went to public school. I had a car or bus ride across town to the Catholic school to join my dozen classmates, ten of whom were boys. We had changed from a neighborhood school in St. Louis that had two classrooms for every grade to a very small school that had two grades in each classroom. I had no friends when I came home, so I cried to my dog, terribly lonely. I felt exiled in my new life. My prayer became a long moan of loneliness.

I remember that, as a family, we were all astonished by the tiny St. John's Church, commenting that it was smaller than the sacristy of St. Luke's in St. Louis. The awe and mystery were gone. It smelled like old dust and creaked and groaned with every footstep. It was heated by floor furnaces, and we had to walk over the grates to get down the aisle. The statues were gaudy with paint. The few little girls struggled with the Latin High Mass in the choir loft, me among them. The few little boys were altar servers. Having experienced the transcendent Mystery through Catholic culture, we had now entered the culture of the minority. No Catholic priest or parishioner visited to welcome us to town or the parish. We were actually told that unless we lived in Tuscaloosa for five generations we were not from there.

Tuscaloosa in the 1950s was stratified by social clubs. This was particularly evident in our neighborhood of doctors, lawyers, and mayors. One was an outcast for life if he or she was not initiated into a sorority or fraternity in the fifth grade, with formal dances and long ball gowns, all starting in elementary school. My parents had both felt the abuse of such a system when they were in college in Manhattan, Kansas. They were both farm kids and were shunned by the town sorority and fraternity students. Now they were strong in their stand that, as a family, we stood on our own integrity, not on what the neighbors thought. They said that most of the people of Tuscaloosa thought the world ended at the city limits. They assured us that the real world was a lot bigger.

Those were very difficult years for my family. Daddy was a chemist and worked for Wood Treating Chemicals Company, traveling the entire southeast. He left home on Monday morning, traveled all week, and returned on Friday evening. My little sister, Rose Ann, ran and hid each Monday morning, not wanting to see him leave. Mother toughed it out, but I could tell it was hard on her to have to make decisions alone all week. We had several medical emergencies. A month or so after our move, I was in great abdominal pain and had to have an emergency appendectomy. John was found on the road one night beside his bicycle. He had been on his way to a boy scout meeting. Within a few days he had a convulsion at home and we learned he had epilepsy.

Mother was not to be outdone by any of these circumstances. I remember two deliberate things she did in response. When she married and moved away from her family in Kansas she experienced great loneliness raising small children in relative isolation. Now in Tuscaloosa she realized that others carried such feelings of abandonment. She began sitting in the very back pew at church so she could spot newcomers. Whoever she saw she greeted after church to find out who they were and where they came from. She shared things going on in the parish that might possibly interest them. She became trusted by pastors and people.

We had no other family in Alabama, but both of my parents had grown up in big families and knew what it felt like with extended family gathered around the table for big holidays. Mother began inviting foreign students from the University of Alabama to join us for Thanksgiving and Christmas, people whose extended families were in other countries. This gave us world family. I remember Myron from the Ukraine and his story of escaping from the Communists, even being pursued by their agents in New York City, where he was stabbed in the back and lost one lung. I remember various couples from several Latin American countries. Our world became larger and more colorful. The face of God for me took on many colors and shapes and tongues. I understood what universal meant in defining Catholic. This is the first time I met God in the stranger, the lonely and sad, the refugee.

From the experience, I knew the table fellowship that Christ imaged in his life with so many of the outcast. By eating with the prostitute, the tax collector, and the leper Jesus was saying that all were one. There was no distinction among persons. Taking from a common dish or cup was a declaration of family. The sign he left with us just before his death was gathering all his friends around the table and telling them to do the same, remembering him in the breaking of the Bread. In Corinthians, the community is chastised because they made distinctions among the people whenever they gathered. They were reminded that all are one Body in Christ. I learned this at our family table, where many different kinds of people were welcomed, their stories shared, and we were made one.

Mother's life example and words taught me not to wallow in my own misfortune, but to get going and do something productive. The antidote to self-pity was to be useful, to be helpful to others, to find a way to see the bigger world and celebrate the gifts of many peoples, many cultures.

Another gift of my own loneliness was that I began to develop interiority. I sought time alone. I remember Mother wondering if I had become a moody teenager. But it was just the inner space that was growing. I was sorting things out. I did change from a loud mouth little kid to a sedate, thoughtful teenager. My sense of the presence of God never waned. I was faithful to prayer, kneeling every night by my bed, often with tears and supplication for friends. God was very real and alive to me, the one who understood my longings, who was the companion of my heart of hearts.

REFLECTION
What were some difficulties you faced as a child? How did you cope?

What developed within you? Perhaps your imagination, an intuitive experience, or a deeper knowing of God?

Describe the outer difficulties and the inner world you found.

Chapter 5: BRIDE OF CHRIST

I have been asked many times how long I have known that I wanted to be a Sister. I think I have always desired it. I cannot remember a time seriously seeing myself in any other way. It was not that I ever had a close friendship during my childhood with any of my teachers who were Sisters, though I admired most of them. It was not because they were good and dedicated teachers. My mother was one of those. But I could see that the entire focus and purpose of their lives was God.

I remember as a teenager writing in my diary, thinking about a boy I was very attracted to. When it came down to it, I knew my life was to be given totally to God, that my heart was in awe and love with the One who had given all to me. I cannot remember any one experience that was a turning point in this direction. It was more as if God glued me together to be "monk," to be a Sister. I was drawn to the silence. I had a sense of the Mystery. Nothing else drew me as strongly. I did not talk about religious life as a child or teenager. Somehow that seemed a bit too goody two-shoes, a bit overly sweet and pious for conversation with my family and friends. But I never wanted anything else. I never loved anyone else as much. God had placed the longing within me. The only reason I could love the Unknowable is that I had already experienced being loved.

Several friends questioned me once I announced that I would enter the monastery the summer after high school. All I could truthfully tell them was from the Baltimore Catechism:

Q: Why did God make you?

A: God made me to know, love, and serve Him, and to be happy with Him in heaven.

I was not so sure about the heaven bit. I couldn't conjure up an image of heaven that was not tinged with boredom, but I wanted to know God more deeply, to love with all my heart and mind and soul, and to serve in whatever way was needed. I went with enthusiasm and deep joy.

I joined the Benedictine Sisters of Cullman, Alabama, at age seventeen after high school. These were the only Sisters I knew at the time. I did not know who Benedict was, nor anything about his Rule. I was not really aware of all the different orders and their varying charisms. In retrospect, this was another total grace because the monastic charism is the one I most fully fit.

I was a very prayerful person as a postulant. After the many hours of chanting the psalms in Latin I knelt and prayed the rosary and other prayers. But our lives were very busy. I was carrying twenty-one hours of college courses, driving to town for the community mail, cleaning floors, and doing whatever else I was told to do. My extra prayers were getting squeezed out. I felt that I had prayed more as a high school student. So I went to Sister Maurus, our novice director, and said I was probably in the wrong place. Probably I needed to be in a cloister for contemplative prayer. Maurus said a lot that day, as she usually did so well, but only one thing stuck in my mind. She told me that after the horrors of World War II a number of monks from St. Bernard went to Gethsemani to be Trappists. One by one each returned to Cullman saying the Trappists were just as busy as they were, but the Trappists made cheese and bread, while the monks at St. Bernard taught boys. If that is how it is, I thought, I might as well do something productive and teach in Alabama where the need was great. So, a very practical reason kept me there.

After nine months as a postulant, we became novices and received the habit of the Benedictine Sisters and the title of Sister. We entered the church in bridal gowns. I reveled in the bridal imagery. I was marrying Christ. Christ had chosen me.

I loved the novitiate courses, diving into sacred scripture, which I was being introduced to for the first time. Sister Maurus, who taught us most of our theology courses, was then completing her master's degree at the Benedictine Institute of Sacred Theology (BIST). She was full of enthusiasm and truly inspired me. I was in my element.

Each Saturday I spent hours preparing for the Sunday Eucharist by reading Pius Pasch's *The Church's Year of Grace.* I pondered the scripture readings and the commentaries on them, as well as the history of each particular season or feast. I lingered with the words and images that struck me. The liturgical season fed my soul: the hope and longing of Advent, the warm feelings of Christmas, the penitential feel of Lent, the deep mysticism of Easter, and the enthusiasm of Pentecost.

As novices we put on productions for the rest of the sisters. I remember organizing one for All Saints Day in which we memorized Psalm 84 and recited it like a Greek chorus. It summarized the fervor I had as a novice. This psalm has meant much to me ever since, summarizing my longing and pure delight to be living in God's house.

How lovely is your dwelling place,
Lord, God of hosts.

My soul is longing and yearning,
is yearning for the courts of the Lord.
My heart and my soul ring out their joy
to God, the living God.

The sparrow herself finds a home
and the swallow a nest for her brood;
she lays her young by your altars,
Lord of Hosts, my king and my God.

They are happy, who dwell in your house,
for ever singing your praise.

They are happy, whose strength is in you,
in whose hearts are the roads to Zion.

As they go through the Bitter Valley
they make it a place of springs
the autumn rain covers it with blessings.
They walk with ever growing strength,
they will see the God of gods in Zion.

O Lord God of hosts, hear my prayer,
give ear, O God of Jacob.
Turn your eyes, O God, our shield,
look on the face of your anointed.

One day within your courts
is better than a thousand elsewhere.
The threshold of the house of God
I prefer to the dwellings of the wicked.

For the Lord God is a rampart, a shield;
he will give us his favor and glory.
The Lord will not refuse any good
to those who walk without blame.

Lord, God of hosts,
Happy the one who trusts in you!
(The Grail translation, Paulist Press, 1966)

At the June annual Community retreat that I attended as a novice, the retreat director, whose name I have long since forgotten, spoke to us about the Sacred Heart of Jesus. This is a mystical image of the heart of Christ exposed with the lance through it and rays of light emanating from it. The pictures or statues of the image did not draw me, but the theology of it was important in my prayer.

At the center of the Mystery of the Incarnation was the fact of Christ's total love for us, poured out, body broken, blood spilled, yearning to give us all. The heart image radiated, alive with the fire of Divine Love. I sensed this love beckoning me into deeper union. During that retreat I remember desiring to live every moment in this heart love of Christ. I walked slowly outside and tried to let each footfall be filled with a sense of the presence of God, walking in wonder and gratitude that I literally lived in God's house, desiring to live each breath in response with full consciousness of this wondrous Love. I lived for several days in an altered state of consciousness with this desire in my soul.

Ponder your own love life with God.

Is there a central image that characterizes it?

Do you have a psalm or a prayer that summarizes the deepest aspects of that relationship?

Maybe you would like to memorize it—"learn it by heart."

Chapter 6: MISS PERFECT

When I was in my twenties I was absolutely perfect. Years later I realized my life journey was divided into decades. There was a significant turning point with a new direction about every ten years. My first ten years were childhood in St. Louis, and the next ten were adolescence in Tuscaloosa.

During the next decade, the 1960s, when I was in my twenties, I was absolutely perfect. With two years at Sacred Heart College in Cullman under my belt, I began teaching fifth and sixth grades at St. Clements in Woodlawn in the fall of 1963. Over the next seven years I did everything I was told and did it perfectly. I taught in a different school in a different place with a different grade, living with a different group of Sisters, each year. Each summer I went to St. Louis University to finish my A.B. with a major in theology and minors in philosophy and education. No vacations were taken in those days.

Wherever we lived at a local parish, we had a small convent beside the school and lived a cloistered life—no car, no visiting, limited shopping for food and group supplies. Each day we conscientiously prayed Lauds and Vespers, and we attended Mass in the parish church. Those were the years of liturgical change with Vatican II, gradually changing all the prayer from Latin to the vernacular (English in our case), and restructuring the prayer to reflect the essential elements as described in early church documents. "Participation" was the big word. We were told to participate in the Liturgy, rather than be observers who often prayed our individual private devotions during Mass. I worked tirelessly to help children and parishioners to understand the changes, to learn hymns in English, and to encourage them to respond to the prayers of the Mass rather than let the prayers be mumbled by the altar servers alone. It was a time of great energy and enthusiastic hope.

In addition to teaching all day, we had packed schedules after school—training altar servers, cleaning the sacristy, tutoring, teaching religion to Catholic children who went to public school, giving music lessons, practicing the organ, training the choir, etc., etc. We sometimes cleaned the school and the church. We, of course, did our own cooking and cleaning in the convent. The Sisters literally did *everything* in the parish. The lay women sometimes helped with altar linens, and the men were ushers and counted the Sunday collection, but little else.

Over the years I have run into various people who have spoken to me about the abuse they received from overly strict, even cruel, sisters who taught them. My response to them has been to explain that these women were abused. With little or no training they were told to do almost anything, and under duress they did it, whether talented or trained or not. Thankfully I never experienced this kind of abuse myself.

This whole system was to change drastically. We were in a unique period of history. Benedictines in the United States, for the most part, had followed the German immigration patterns and did ministry to keep the faith alive among the German immigrants. Cullman was originally a German settlement. By the 1960s there was an attempt to sort out the difference between European customs and the practices essential to the life of a monastery. Imagine getting more than one hundred women to agree about all aspects of their lives! Using the Rule of Benedict as our guide we made monumental changes.

In liturgy, we changed from Latin to English and restructured our entire prayer form. In the 1960's we experimented a lot with the liturgy, often using themes as a focus, offering folk Masses or home liturgies—attempting to make liturgy meaningful to our lives and the lives of the people. Gradually we learned good liturgical principles and found a nourishing daily rhythm.

For Benedictines liturgy is paramount. The Liturgy of the

House is structured to consecrate each part of our day to God. The Rule of Benedict, which dates from the sixth century Roman Empire, directs monastics to pray seven times a day and once in the middle of the night. As women serving the church of Alabama we had been doing this by praying Lauds, Prime, and Terce together in early morning, Sext and None at noon, Vespers and Matins before supper, and Compline after supper. We got it all in, including all 150 psalms each week as suggested by St. Benedict. But there were no pauses for silence. There were very short readings, the same every week. We were not really praying eight different times each day, but four. So we decided to design four quality prayer periods: Lauds, Noon Prayer, Vespers, and Compline, adding Vigil on Saturday nights or preceding any big feast. We added silent pauses after each psalm and a period of longer silence after the reading. We developed cycles of readings so we would hear more of Sacred Scripture.

We made many other changes in our lives. In dress, we decided it was essential to dress simply and modestly, but each sister could decide on her own wardrobe, usually recycled clothing. Our ring would be the outward sign of our commitment, as it was for married women. We continued to turn in to the treasurer all money we earned, but we each received $25 a month for clothing and personal supplies. Before the changes, we had knelt to ask for each bar of soap or tube of toothpaste we needed.

At that time my life's project was to do absolutely everything as perfectly as possible. I prayed at the appropriate times, and more if I could fit it in. My prayer was fervent, primarily a cry for help just to survive. I worked hard. We all worked hard. I did everything I was told. I was on time, modest, and efficient. My drawers were neat, after all, I was a nun. And I had an ulcer! The doctor scolded and told me I was not a machine. My Sisters Raphael and Loretta, with whom I lived and worked, worried that they had done something wrong or had not done enough. The illness turned out to be a gift. It allowed me to listen within. I had prayed more as a teenager. I had time then to daydream and enjoy solitude. No more! I was always producing—primarily teaching. Imagine all the energy it took for an introvert to be transplanted annually. I was dried up within. Like most workaholics, I had neglected my love life. I had denied the Voice calling me within.

I really longed for a way to calm my over-thinking mind, to find a teacher to help me learn to meditate, to enter the silence in a deeper way as the mystics had done. There was no teacher. It was implied that mysticism was for the "real contemplatives," those who lived in cloisters, the Trappists and Carmelites. In those days we rose at 5:00 a.m., dressed, and went to the chapel by 5:20 for twenty minutes of "meditation" before the group Morning Praise. I looked around to see how to meditate, and saw the other sisters reading spiritual books. So I followed their example and read spiritual books each day. This was another mental exercise for me. I did learn about spiritual things, but I longed for a deeper prayer. I nurtured that longing, somehow knowing that the longing itself had been placed within me by God.

REFLECTION
What type of prayer feeds your soul?
Listen within.

What prayer form can help you keep centered in God as you begin each day? During your workday? As you conclude your day?

Are you drawn to pray at sunrise and sunset? Try it.

There are many books available today for praying the Liturgy of the Hours with a simple morning and evening prayer. Some are for one week, and some have a four-week cycle of psalms and readings.

Reflection

The basic format for our Lauds and Vespers in Cullman is
the following:
>Call to worship
>Hymn
>Two or three psalms – different ones each day on a four
>week cycle
>Canticle from Hebrew Scripture in morning and from
>Christian Scripture in evening
>Reading from Scripture – two year cycle
>Canticle of Zachary (Luke 1:68-79) in the morning and
>Canticle of Mary (Luke 1:46-55) in the evening.
>Intercessory prayer for the needs of our world
>Concluding prayer

Chapter 7: THE GROPERS

In 1970 more great changes began to happen to encourage me on the inner journey. I went to a Pre-Chapter of the Federation of St. Scholastica as an "Under Thirty Responder." Here I met the great women of Benedictine renewal who were now asking the young women in their communities to give them some feedback on what they had written and how they were attempting to redefine American Benedictine life. I was put on a committee with Johnette Putnam and Joan Chittister to help write a position paper for the Federation titled "Prophetic Faith Community." Joan had just received her doctorate from the University of Pennsylvania. Johnette and her community were taking a public stand against segregation in Louisiana. I was deeply inspired by these women and set on fire with the concepts they were putting forth as we poured through the Gospels and the 1500-year-old Rule of Benedict, seeking to redefine how we wished to live them today.

At the meeting I met and heard Brother Frank of Taize and Benedictine Brother David Steindl-Rast for the first time. During the following year I helped Frank relocate in Atlanta where I was working. I was deeply influenced by this group of Taize Brothers, living among the poor, doing ordinary jobs, living a life of prayer and community. In those years David was encouraging and helping sisters around the country set up Houses of Prayer. He came and gave our annual retreat and stayed to orient eleven of us into a month-long House of Prayer Experience in Benet Hall. As these two men talked, my desire for prayer and contemplation was rekindled. It had always been part of me, but in my need to be perfect, I had responded to the call of mythic membership in a religious community and just poured myself into the tasks I was assigned. They were good tasks, very important ministries of education, but I had not given equal time to my inner journey. I had neglected my love life.

The House of Prayer Experience was a turning point for me. We had help from several experts. But mostly there was unstructured time *to be*. Then the unexpected happened. Just when I had all that I longed for, time for prayer and a group to support that effort, I was unable to pray. I was not even able to organize and lead our simple group morning or evening prayer when it was my turn. I was in a funk, unable to shake off the low mood or to produce anything. The others in the group were very patient with me. A climax came on an outing at Smith Lake. I just floated away from the group one day on an inner tube—finally facing and struggling with my compulsive self. Would I ever be good enough? No! Would I ever deserve to be loved? No! That had absolutely nothing to do with God's great love for me. Could I just receive that love? I couldn't figure out how to do this. Spiritual writers told me it had something to do with dying to self, and I had been trying to do that. In one moment of awareness I realized I was trying to commit spiritual suicide. We do not make death happen, even dying to self. It happens to us. It is a Mystery much larger than self.

Within the next few days I felt a breaking open at a liturgy with Father Larry Hein. I had an overwhelming experience of God loving me just exactly as I was, bare bones. I could let go of my need to be perfect, to do it all right, even to figure out how to receive correctly. I could let go of the galoshes of perfectionism. What a freedom! What a grace!

I notice this kind of angst often comes around age thirty. Not just, "Who am I?" but "Who is this 'I' that is such a miserable creature?" We wonder why we are so miserable but have no answer. It is easy to project it on others. There may or may not be anything in the external world that is upsetting us. One is just in a snit, a funk. Finally at this seeming impasse, with an inbreaking, one can finally get in touch with her soul. One becomes opened to *the* story, to the divine Mystery that is bigger that one's ego-controlled little self. Then we utter a deep "yes," even when there is not even a question that has been articulated.

During the early sixties large numbers of young women were entering convents and monasteries around the country. The whole country, if not the world, was in major social flux. By the late sixties and early seventies large numbers were leaving convents. Many of my good friends left with this Exodus. This was very difficult. I knew I was not staying to be a teacher, a principal, or a religious education director. I had done all those things, and I had primarily succeeded in them by worldly standards. But, really, almost anyone could do those things. I knew I stayed to be monastic, to put God and the God-relationship central to my life, to live committed to others who had this same vision. So the next ten years, the decade of my thirties, became a *most* serious search for monastic renewal.

After the summer House of Prayer a group of us met monthly to discuss what an experimental monastic house would be like. A month in the summer was not enough. A purposeful prayer orientation was supposed to be the center of our lives as monastics. I felt the need for deeper study on the topic and went to graduate school at St. John's in Collegeville, Minnesota, for a master's in liturgy and monastic studies. While I was in Minnesota the group continued meeting in Cullman, working out the practical details of our dream.

We made plans to live in an ordinary neighborhood, to focus on prayer and community, while letting work take a back seat for a while. Our ministry was to pray and to live community. For the very practical reason of finding suitable work, we planned to locate in Birmingham. We called ourselves "the Gropers," purposely choosing a name that said we did not have all the answers and were not on some exalted path, but we were seeking, exploring, dreaming. We had never heard the word used in any other context. We were all around thirty years old. Sister Maurus continued as our mentor in the planning stages and when we moved to Birmingham, but we had no elders living among us to show us the way, just our own enthusiasm and earnestness.

This became the most formative experience of my life, and ultimately the most painful. It was formative because we had to articulate as clearly as possible our dream. We diligently studied the renewal papers that had just been issued by the Federation of St. Scholastica, especially "Eucharistic Ecclesiola" and "Prophetic Faith Community." We wanted to be "a church in miniature," as described by those documents. We desired to live like the church in Acts of the Apostles. As our whole Community was renewing with Vatican II we were reclaiming our monastic identity. We identified prayer and community as the two essential foundation stones. Ministry was then to flow out of the dynamic of prayer and community life, responding to the needs of the people in the area where we lived and standing against the false values of our society.

We Gropers took this most seriously as we set our goals. To honor prayer as primary we decided that each of us would have half the day in solitude, and we would gather for morning Lauds and evening Vespers. To have strong community life we coordinated our schedules so we could have extended time around the supper table every night. We shared all in common and lived most simply. We challenged one another strongly and constantly. It is the most authentic living situation I have ever experienced.

We were diligent with our prayer, taking turns to be creative within a daily rhythm of Lauds and Vespers. During my period of perfectionism and frenetic activity I had viewed our daily Benedictine prayer as another work that I had to do, one that I did *for* God—singing the psalms in praise or lament, praying for the needs of the world. The Rule of Benedict calls the Liturgy of the Hours *Opus Dei*, and I had translated that "work *for* God."

As Gropers we introduced a subtle but significant change. We synchronized our community prayer with sunrise and sunset, changing by five minutes every few days with the sun. It was as if we were responding to the Mystery. That had a deep effect on me. I realized we were praying and playing the work *of* God, as if God

34

were conducting a great symphony of praise, and in awe we were caught in the tide, the rise and the fall of sun (the Son). I found a story that told about a rooster that used to be very responsible. He had the awesome responsibility to crow each morning to make the sun rise. One morning he overslept. Lo and behold! The sun rose by itself. In the future he crowed in response to this wonder each morning. This is what the Liturgy of the Hours became for me. A response to the Mystery.

We made a very special event of Eucharist. We invited a different priest each week, so as not to wear out any one person. Bishop Vath came sometimes. We made it a full evening experience of Eucharist, then had dinner and lively discussion, often inviting neighbors to join us. This was our way to extend the Table of the Lord into fuller human table fellowship.

But the really formative part for me was having half of each day for private prayer. There were six of us in three bedrooms. Half worked in the morning and half in the afternoon, so each had bedroom space alone for half the day. We also had a chapel or the front porch for solitude. Primarily each of us did *Lectio Divina* faithfully with the lectionary readings of the day or spiritual reading from the spiritual masters. I also shared with the group what I thought were tasty morsels from some of the courses I had just taken at St. John's.

By being faithful to daily solitude I was shifted and changed, cared for and broken open. Primarily I sat with the daily scripture in *lectio* mode. I remember so many mornings sitting on the front porch swing facing Highland Golf Course, listening to the birds. I mulled on the Word of the day, chewed the cud of it, savored any fragrance within it. I came to see how the Word judged me, not in any condemning sense, but rather in God's power to set me right, to open my eyes in subtle but real ways, to shift my heart, to knock me off my feet and put me upright. It wooed and wowed me. It allowed me to be touched by God's gracious action. It was like water pouring over stone, drip by drip, until the stone of my soul was worn smooth.

I had looked forward to this free time so much because my life had formerly been so driven by ministry. I had enjoyed each of the ministries I had been involved in. By that time I had already been an elementary and junior high teacher, a principal, and a religious education director. But it was unrelenting work and constant pressure. I expected that once freed from the pressure, I would be a better person. But this did not happen. In fact my impatience and negativity, criticalness and perfectionism almost seemed to become more pronounced. But now I more easily saw them for what they were, named them, and struggled with them. I remember being deeply struck by the Good News that Jesus saved us when we were sinners, when we were at our worst. It was about God loving us, healing us poor, feeble critters. It would be Bad News if I had to do it all and make myself perfect. I had already been there, and that project had created an ulcer in me. But it was about God's gracious love.

I remember one day having a confrontation with my compulsive self. I used to get an internal image of smoothness when things were running well, and would see an interior image almost like unwrinkled paper with a white felt-like feel. But when things were at odds within myself I internally felt and saw crinkled paper, splotches of black and white, and felt a squirming dis-ease in my solar plexus. That day within a few moments these two images and feelings battled within me, going from one to the other, back and forth. Then it all dissipated, and I have been free from that particular inner struggle ever since with its accompanying feeling of squirminess. Compulsions still appear, but fairly rapidly I can face them, recognize them for what they are, and laugh in their face.

It was at this time I started the practice of Yoga. I was looking for someone who could teach me to meditate, to quiet my mind, and to enjoy just sitting in God's presence. I did not find a teacher of meditation, but Priscilla Lovoy graciously taught us Hatha Yoga. Only later did I realize how much I needed Hatha Yoga to get my body grounded before I could ever begin to meditate. Each week we learned to breathe and stretch and relax. I had lived my life so much in my head. This practice of stretching and releasing and being aware of the stretch and the release brought me home within the Temple of my body, this Temple where God had chosen to live. It helped me learn to be respectful in a new way to the Incarnation—God coming into this earthly, fleshy condition. Yoga has continued to be the best help to get me in touch with my body, to release tension, and to prepare me for prayer. I remember pondering how important it was to have a teacher to learn these physical movements. I wondered where there was anyone to teach me about entering the vast space of the soul. Silence and solitude were my teachers. They are primarily what I continue to seek to this day when I need to return to my true self.

Each of us worked only half the day. We lived in a deteriorating neighborhood and did whatever kind of work we could find nearby. I was a typist. The first year I worked for Highland Racquet Club and the second for Medicenter across the street. Karen sold Avon and met all the lonely old women in the neighborhood. Later she worked at Pasquales Pizza, then pumped gas at Contorno's Gulf. Yvette went out in her short red and gold dress to work at Burger King, then worked at Pasquales Pizza, and then helped at the Workshop with handicapped adults. Felice, Edwina, and Renee all taught half a day, Felice with kindergarten, Edwina and Renee sharing fourth grade. Later, Magdalena and Madeline joined us, and they both taught. We had a rhythm going with the use of only two cars. The dream, like Taize's, was to live very simply (half a small closet each), to do regular work in the neighborhood, and to identify with the poor. We realized immediately we could not really identify with the poor because we were educated. We were white. We only had to open our mouths and any employer would readily hire us. Yet, each of us had periods of unemployment, and the sense of failure and uselessness was felt and examined.

Our work is what got us in trouble with other community members. The fact that we had part-time work and that half of us were not in church ministry was a *major* sore spot, especially the fact that we were all so young and able. It came down to an issue about money and whether we were carrying our fair share. One sister stated, "What right do the Gropers have to tell us about prayer? They make us earn all the money."

Actually, it was miraculous that we were allowed to try this experience in the first place. Religious around the world had been called by Vatican II to return to the spirit of their founders and to listen for and address the signs of the times. Houses of women religious in the United States took this admonition most seriously. These women, who had single-handedly started schools or built hospitals, who went to some of the worst spots doing social work, had usually done all of this work with very little education backing them up. The Sister Formation Movement of the 1950s worked nationally to get Sisters educated professionally and to train some of their members theologically so they could form others within their communities with more scriptural spirituality and theological grounding. In Cullman we were in step with the times, perhaps ahead of many other houses. Our leaders had always held education as paramount and sent us to the best schools in the United States for training in our selected fields. A substantial amount of money had been spent on us. Our Sisters wanted a return on their investment.

I have already mentioned some of the changes that came for women religious with Vatican II. In my estimation, the greatest change was in the way we interpreted and practiced obedience. The pre-Vatican II way was for the superior to make *all* decisions and give orders that covered *absolutely every* aspect of our lives, large and mundane. Every summer at the end of retreat we each received from the Prioress a slip of paper with our obedience for the year. It told us what school we would teach in and which grade we would teach, sometimes telling us to do things for which we had no talent or preparation. By the 1970s as a community we opted for "open placement," making it the responsibility of the Sister to discern her best talents and seek the best place to serve, all in dialogue with the Prioress. It called us to prayer and a deep listening to the voice of the Holy Spirit. It called us to know ourselves better, to be open to criticism and comment by the Prioress, and to take responsibility for our decisions. It was also the point at which we began branching out into many different kinds of ministries beyond teaching.

Before Vatican II almost all group decisions were made by the Prioress. Now as a community we had many, many meetings and worked for a consensus before moving in any direction as a group. It was a real learning process to be civil to one another, much less to come to an agreement about major aspects of our lives together. We learned to listen to the voice of the Spirit within each sister and to trust the group wisdom. The outcome was always different and better than any one person's original viewpoint. All this took a lot of suffering and pain as we challenged each other and grew and changed and continued serving in so many ways.

The Gropers entered this dialogue process. We were asked to report at regular intervals to the Community Council about our goals and how we were living them out. This was very stressful, but it caused us to do our own continuous sorting and challenging of one another about every aspect of our lives. We constantly witnessed the Spirit at work in all our processing.

The Gropers came during a time of monumental transition in the church. It was one attempt in the sorting and discerning process with our community. The basic question that we posed was: Where is our primary life energy directed? Is it focused on prayer? Or is the focus on our work? The honest answer has always been "on our work." As a foundation we had left cloisters of Germany and came as immigrants into a hostile territory. Our ministry was primary. It still is. It is what drives every one of us at Sacred Heart. Prayer does definitely have an important place in our daily lives, but our ministry is our élan vital, our driving force. As a community we are very good, very conscientious, and very faithful church worker women, responding to all kinds of needs.

The Groper years were a most important two years of my life. I was given space to shift from a workaholic to a monastic with a contemplative center. My values were articulated more clearly. It allowed God to cleanse my heart and mold me in new life forms.

REFLECTION

The *Lectio Divina* **method** that I used on the front porch swing I call "slow motion reading of the Bible." This method, that Benedictines have used through the ages, has four traditional steps:

Lectio – Read a short text slowly and prayerfully

> Allow yourself to be calmed down and opened to the wonder of God. Then choose a text. The Sacred Scripture is the primary text, but any reading that helps you enter the God presence is fine. The longest text you would ever want to use is the length of a liturgical reading, but even shorter is wonderful. Read it slowly and reverently. Read the text aloud. Listen to it. Slow your whole body down to slow motion. Note any word or phrase that especially speaks to your soul.

Meditatio – Ponder in your heart any phrase that draws you

> This is a deep listening phase. Spend time on the section that really strikes you, that draws you, that entices you. Monastic literature uses lots of digestive terms in speaking about *meditatio*: savor the morsel, let the aroma tickle the nostrils, chew the cud of the meaty part, digest it thoroughly. Do not be in a hurry. Linger and enjoy as long is any sense is enticed.

Oratio – Pray the deepest prayer of your heart

> However your heart is moved, express that to God. God has spoken to you during *lectio* and *meditation*. Now what do you want to express to your Divine Lover? It may be in a silent yearning or a formal prayer. It may be expressed in art form of poetry or drawing. The important thing is the growing relationship with God. Give it time.

Contemplatio – Linger in the deep inner space with the One who loves you. Rest in God. Let God love you. Extend the silent communion as you feel so invited.

41

Lectio **with your own life drama**—do some deep pondering:

What were your early adult dreams?

In what ways did the reality not measure up to your dream?

What were the struggles involved?

What were the obstacles?

Where was the Voice of God for you?

Chapter 8: DARKNESS

After two years as Gropers we all went in various directions. Edwina, Renee, and Yvette left the community entirely, but they each made the decision with self-knowledge and without bitterness. I was asked to become Formation Director in charge of the training of our new members and to be Community Secretary in Cullman. The other Gropers moved to Cullman or took ministry positions elsewhere.

During my first year as Formation Director for our community, several women came and left in short order, or they said they were coming and never arrived. So there was no one in the Formation program. I spent my time as Vocation Director. I tried to keep my rhythm of prayer, but everyone around me spent her primary energy in ministry, so there was not the same support for what I considered essential. It also created a great dilemma within me. How could I be in charge of forming new members if my priorities were different from the rest of the community? Either I had to teach what I considered essential and be at odds with the rest of the community, or I had to teach what they were living and feel at odds within myself. After a year I resigned as Formation Director. I knew in all honesty I could not divide my soul. I did continue as Vocation Director, deciding I could be an initial contact as women came to discern if this was the life God called them to.

This was some of the darkest time of my life. The community and way of life I had always embraced so enthusiastically, I now felt at odds with. I railed against God: "How can you place such a strong desire for prayer and contemplation within me and then frustrate it? If you are calling me to a life of deeper prayer, show me how to do that. Every structure to support this desire has failed. I do not know what to do or where to find it." I had really worked myself into a knot over this dilemma, and God wasn't giving any answer.

43

I remember talking with saintly Father Paschal Botz, a monk of St. John's in Collegeville, when he gave us a community retreat. His advice was to wait for five years. He said if I had an authentic call it would still be there. If not, I would find other directions. FIVE YEARS! That was a lifetime to me in my thirties. He also said when someone is young with a cause they are called stubborn. When they are old, they are said to have character.

One important help I received at the time was an introduction to Zen meditation. (It must be true that when the disciple is ready the master will appear.) I was able to attend an eight-day retreat with Father Oshida, a Japanese Dominican priest. He had been invited by Professor Lucien Miller to teach Zen to his prayer group in Spencer, Massachusetts. Others were invited in order to help cover the cost of bringing him from Japan. Oshida had the twenty-some of us sit on the floor for thirty-minute periods focusing on each exhale. Then we all stood, walked slowly around the meditation hall, and sat down for another thirty-minute period. We did this sequence several times a day. The total silence and stillness enticed me. We stayed in total silence for the whole week, even as we were sent off in various directions for a couple hours of manual labor every day.

I worked really hard to get this prayer right. By the third day I was working so hard I was ready to pop, ready to jump up, run out of the room, and scream. I peeked and looked at the others, whom I had learned at introductions had never done any meditation before, nor any yoga. My pride kept me on my cushion. "If they can do it, I can do it!" Then something shifted within me beyond my doing, and I let go. I just sat. No effort. No big experience of the presence of God. But just sat. At some point I noticed the forest creatures, the birds and bugs making their sounds, the wind in the leaves. Harmony. All one.

I had a chance to talk about my dream and my life conflicts with Basil Pennington who had come down the street from his monastery to attend the retreat. I also had a conference with Oshida. Later I got a ride with him to Weston Priory. Weston is a community of Benedictine monks who had innovative renewal going on in Vermont. Oshida gave them a retreat, and I enjoyed the Vermont woods. On my last day there he asked to see me and told me, "Yes, it is possible—this monastic form you seek. It is living at Weston." That was all well and good, but I did not live in Weston. I lived in Cullman. I still suffered with my dilemma—how to find a more contemplative life structure.

The Zen meditation form I learned from Oshida became my prayer form for life. The silence and stillness drew me. It was an antidote to my headiness—to sit and breathe and know that I was breathing, part of the Breath of God. It offered me a breakthrough in prayer. When returning to Cullman I rose before dawn each day and sat overlooking our lake to do Zen meditation before community prayer.

I had many conversations with my Prioress, Sister Patricia Ann. She was totally bewildered about what to do with me, and how to respond to yet more of my peers who were leaving the community. She did admit to a conversion within herself. She said when she had entered the monastery, she did so to teach. She considered contemplation to be for cloistered religious—for Trappists or Carmelites. But with renewal she had changed her mind and could now claim that monasticism and contemplation were our heritage as Benedictines. But she did not say how this could be lived out.

I read a passage from Merton at this time. He had been struggling with his abbot about the desire to go to the hermitage full-time and about his writing about peace. Some of his words resonated:

"So you will ask me: how do I reconcile obedience, true obedience (which is synonymous with love) with a situation like this? Shouldn't I just blast the whole thing wide open, or walk out, or tell them to jump in the lake?

...I am where I am. I have freely chosen this state, and have freely chosen to stay in it when the question of a possible change arose. If I am a disturbing element, that is all right. I am not making a point of being that, but simply of saying what my conscience dictates and doing so without seeking my own interest...

...We have got to be aware of the awful sharpness of the truth when it is used as a weapon, and since it can be the deadliest weapon, we must take care that we don't kill more than falsehood with it. In fact we must be careful how we 'use' truth, for we are ideally the instruments of truth and not the other way around."

(*Thomas Merton, Prophet in the Belly of a Paradox,* 1978, p. 28 and 38)

The conflict became so great within me that I knew I needed to look beyond Cullman. I asked to spend a year at Still Point House of Prayer outside Albany, New York. I went in the fall of 1978. In the early weeks there I felt like a novice again. I wrote my family and friends on October 24, 1978:

"We are located on a 30-acre farm between Lake Saratoga and the Hudson River. From a hill down the road one can see the Adirondack Mts. to the northwest and the Green Mts. of Vermont to the east—gorgeous! The fall has been spectacular.

"The house of prayer has been in existence for almost seven years, but within the last two years this big old farm house has been bought and renovated—simply but aesthetically done—with unfinished pine for all woodwork, giving a rustic look. The chapel is paneled in the same wood and has a round window behind the altar that looks into the forest. There are eight women here for the year, but there is room for many more people to come for short retreats, visits, or counseling.

"Our day begins before dawn with yoga postures, followed

46

by Morning Praise which includes a 45-minute silent meditation period and the proclamation of the Gospel for the day. Breakfast and lunch are 'pick up' style. A respectful silence is kept during the day as each one pursues religious study and does some daily manual labor. The Eucharist is celebrated three mornings, and on Sunday the group celebrates at a nearby parish or at New Skete, a Byzantine Franciscan monastery. Three times a week classes are held on some religious topic. The eight of us who are here for the year earn our living by doing housework twenty hours a week in a residential area 20-30 minutes driving distance away. This work was chosen as a relatively simple way to earn an income while maintaining a quieted mind and heart. Use of the Jesus Prayer is the thread running throughout the day. At 5:30 we gather for some yoga relaxation or chanting and another period of silent meditation. Supper is the time for sharing and general recreation, laughter, and fun. We linger over a unique variety of vegetarian dishes—all delicious. Vespers, which is held around 8:00, is full of rich ritual—processions, candles, incense, song and silence, prayer for the whole Church and the world.

"Perhaps my greatest apprehension in coming here was wondering what kind of people I would be spending the year with. A greater group cannot be found. The spirit of enthusiasm and light-heartedness, the balance of down-to-earth-ness and spiritual thrust, the openness and fun have made me feel totally at home. Sister Sylvia Rosell is the director, a true spiritual leader. She continually challenges us to explore more honestly the Mystery of God, to surrender all parts of our life to Him. Others are from New Orleans, New Jersey, New York, and Alabama.

"We have an acre or so of garden to supply most of our vegetarian needs…The rest of the acreage is forest, which we keep out of right now since hunting season on deer has begun.

"The three hermitages are well built with all the conveniences. They have been occupied since I got here by individuals on ten to thirty day retreats. Sylvia directs them. The reason for some hermit time is to have the real silence and solitude necessary to face one's self, to name the inner demons, to be purified and healed, and thus to be able to hear the Lord more clearly with the ear of the heart. Hermits do get to eat, but no talking except with the director.

"As you can probably tell, I am truly in my element here. This is exactly the atmosphere I was seeking. After being here and getting acquainted for six weeks there will be an evaluation to determine if it would be productive for me to remain for a whole year. The goodness of God overwhelms me in giving me so much. Without having visited before or really knowing all the angles of what I was getting into, I find that this more than meets my hopes. Now it is up to God and me to get going on the hard part of purification. I already feel a great healing going on. I look forward to the adventure that lies ahead."

Little did I know the adventure that did lie ahead—and the purification. At that moment I had the feeling that God had taken me by the hair of the head and placed me in *exactly* what I had been dreaming about. He did. And rubbed my nose in it.

My troubles began when I made the step from visitor to member of the core community. Sister Sylvia had dreamed Still Point. She had the chutzpas to pull it off: to find the farm, to gather the members, and to structure the life. She ran the house and did so as the total authority of the strong Cuban she was. On a daily basis she made rather arbitrary decisions about each of the members in the house and what each one was to do for that day. She and I gradually locked horns. It made me remember my own early days in my monastery with some of our local superiors who were not very psychologically balanced. In my enthusiasm as a young sister I had tried really hard to see Christ in them as Benedict says to do. I had tried to obey all their commands. I had a real sorting out to find my own inner authority and to realize when someone in charge was imbalanced. It is a fine line, because the bottom line is that we

48

ultimately have to die to self and self-will—but we are not supposed to be killed by an obedience that is psychologically unhealthy. I knew I did not need to fight that battle again in this place.

But I had been given the year to explore, so in mid-February I left on the bus and visited several groups who were starting new Benedictine endeavors. Some who were inspired by the Rule of Benedict had never lived in a monastery before, but were trying. Yes, that ancient Rule had the essence and the flexibility to be lived today. I was inspired.

I also stopped in Dallas, Pennsylvania, for a thirty-day retreat with the Mercy Sisters. Sister Cor Mariae, my director, had me sit in Zen several times a day, lengthening the time of sitting as the month went on. The confusion about my dilemma intensified. "What do I do? How do I do it? Where can I find the structure for contemplative living?" Cor suggested I was in a dark night of the soul. I had heard the expression, but I had never read much about it. It sounded like too fancy a phrase for my state of turmoil.

One day as I walked in the woods after an ice storm, I walked down a path no one else had walked. I marveled at all the trees and bushes layered in crystal. At that moment the way the sun was shining on it all was phenomenal, presenting a glittering, sparkling, absolutely marvelous winter display. Ice covered each branch, glistening in the sunlight. Snow diamonds sparkled on the ground. Dark fluff clouds raced across the sun, now hiding its play on the hoarfrost, now a round form surrounded by darkness, now blinking the eye. I stood at the edge of the forest looking into the landfill meadow, overcome by the beauty, taken into loving arms of Life. I stood in awe and thought: "I am the only one to be in this spot today at this time to see this. AAH! I receive it with the deepest gratitude. If I were not here, there would be no one to witness this. I am here to be here. I am here to see. To be a witness to a wonder far beyond any of my doing. The most *I can do* is to use the tiny muscles of my eyelids and open my eyes… Down the road a bit another part of me said, "And for God's sake, stop worrying about the damn galoshes!"

In my journal I wrote, "I thought and planned to run elsewhere so I could realize my dream. Gradually there was a dawning that there was nowhere I could really go to make my dream work, for then I would simply be building my own tower. The Lord is here and will be encountered where and when he desires to reveal himself. No fancy project can tease him into coming. I simply need to wait and be silent. He is coming as a silent early dawn morning. Sometimes leaving much yet in colors of gray, but having shown enough light to be most positive that *He is coming.* I don't recall a moment I ever felt totally without him but this experience has deepened me, humbled me, established an even stronger base in God.

I came north in the autumn days of leaves just beginning to turn.
The glory and brilliance of leaves and life here astonished me,
blinded me with its circus and fireworks.

Then they fell, pools around the trees,
wisps caught in the breeze, the illusion of life blown apart.
The trees stood in their nakedness, hard against the cold blasts,
dark twisted images against the sky.
I have shivered and felt the cold and loneliness.

Yet I do not fear.
A greater mystery is so present and powerfully felt.
The nights are long.
The winter promises only to vent its fury.

But the trees still stand present to *this* moment,
Unashamed of being unclothed and unproductive,
simply waiting
deeply enrooted in mother earth.

How can they be so patient?
They have no awareness that spring and summer will eventually
come.
They simply stand,
arms upraised praising their Creator.
They praise because it is winter dark
and hidden mysteries are being worked.
I praise you, Mysterious One, with the trees."

I ended the retreat knowing I needed to return to the red clay of Alabama. I did not know why. I did not know what. I felt totally homeless. I really identified with the scripture about Jesus, "Foxes have dens and the birds of the air have nests, but the Son of Man has nowhere to lay his head." (Luke 9:60) I had been hollowed out. There was no cozy or warm spot to which I could look forward to sooth my pain.

REFLECTION
What has been the hardest struggle in your life?

How was the God presence made known to you?
What was your response?

Chapter 9: REFUGEES

Meanwhile back in Cullman, my Sisters were planning my future, and unknowingly helping begin another major decade shift. On my way back to the South in May I stopped at my parents' home in Alexandria, Virginia. They had left Alabama in 1960, one month after I entered the monastery. While in Virginia that May I received a letter from Sister Patricia Ann asking me to be Treasurer for a few months. Our college had just closed. All was in transition, and there was some sorting to do. What did I know about finances? Next to nothing. Though I had survived on $600 for the whole past year, half that going for the 30-day retreat.

I also got a phone call from Sister Anne. She said, "Since you don't have anything to do, we want you to coordinate the resettlement of some Vietnamese refugees. We have decided to sponsor a family of thirteen. Any day now they are going to arrive."

I was stunned. Didn't they know what I had been about for the last ten years? No, they really did not have a clue! I stomped and fumed.

I returned to Alabama, and I did both tasks. The Treasurer's position lasted only a few months. I guess I did not make too big a mess. Then the Ngo family arrived. My life totally changed. God said, "Enough of this hand wringing and whining, Mary. It is time to open your eyes wider. Go out to my world. My people are in need."

I learned that the family was Chinese, and that their name was Wu. Ngo was the Vietnamese translation on their legal papers since birth, so that is the name with which they entered our country. The family consisted of the elderly parents, the oldest son and his wife and five children, and the four youngest daughters. Each of the thirteen family members had very different life needs. There was no one else to help them, so I responded, no lofty motive in me. We housed the family on the front campus at St. Bernard Abbey in a now vacant faculty house. One of our former college faculty members had become a reporter at The Cullman Times. She came out one day looking for a story. What better story to tell the people of Cullman than about the boat people. We had all seen these pitiful people on the news each night. She did a wonderful article on the front page of the town newspaper, including photos.

One Saturday a week or so later we had a giant yard sale at the monastery to clean out unwanted furniture. Thousands of people came, hoping for priceless antiques, little knowing we mostly operated with army surplus from Atalla. The little refugee children ran around all day serving lemonade.

That night at 10:00 when I was in the bathtub, Maurus came calling some foolishness at me. At last I heard what she was saying, "St. Bernard just got a threatening phone call: 'A bomb is going off in thirty minutes, and the Vietnamese are going up with it.'" Four of us sisters jumped into one car and zoomed over to their house on the St. Bernard campus. Somehow we stuffed everyone into the car with us. As we drove onto our grounds I thought, "O my God! The bomb is really here at our home. Thousands of people were here all day and saw the children." Folks in Cullman are always mixed up about St. Bernard Abbey (the men's community) and Sacred Heart Monastery (the women's community).

No bomb went off that night, though there was fear ever after that. We had a quick community meeting to ask if we should endanger our "old sisters" by moving the family onto our campus. It was our elders who declared strongly, "We fought the Klan in the old days. We'll fight them again!" (In the 1920s a Klansman had shot and killed Father Coyle on the front porch of St. Paul's Rectory in downtown Birmingham. One of our convents was also burned down in Pratt City.) So we moved the family onto our grounds where they could live in a little house behind our large buildings and be more protected.

There were a total of three refugee families in Cullman, two small families sponsored by St. Paul Lutheran Church and ours. We helped two of the men get jobs at Nicholson File. Unknown to me, Klansmen glared at them at the door of the plant each morning and afternoon, while the Asians bowed and smiled. Then the Klansmen began following them after work and telling them to leave town, saying that they were taking American jobs. Finally one day a Klansman drew a knife during the encounter and threatened to kill them if they did not leave town. Only then did Mr. Em Tien Ngo, who was the eldest son and head of the household we sponsored, tell me what had happened. He had not spoken earlier because he did not want to cause any more trouble for us. I responded, "They wouldn't dare do anything!" He humbly reminded me, "I know about KKK. I hear about KKK in Vietnam."

Cullman had always had a reputation for being a Ku Klux Klan stronghold. I had thought that was in the past. Now I had no idea if the police could be trusted. I called Brian Buegler who had worked in our college but was then at the Sheriff's office. Brian assured me that Sheriff Wendell Roden was clean. He had fired one man in reserves when he learned he was in the Klan. The next day the sheriff's detectives and the FBI arrived. Em Tien identified the two men from photos taken during a recent trial. The man who pulled the knife was a leader in the Cullman clavern. He was arrested, tried, and convicted on federal civil rights charges. He was sentenced to prison for eight months and fined. At that time there was a presidential order out to quell any violence directed at the refugees after the killing of Vietnamese fishermen off the coast of Texas.

The Ngo family lived with us for two years. In Vietnam they had endured the threat of death every day under Communism. They had lived in Bac Lieu on the southern tip of South Vietnam, a wealthy family owning two rice mills, a fruit plantation, and two homes. Everything was confiscated when the North Vietnamese took control on April 30, 1975. After several years of worsening conditions with many friends sent to "reeducation" camps, they fled on a shrimp boat with 106 relatives and a pilot who did not know how to run a boat. After four days and nights in the South China Sea, where they endured a storm and the threat of Thai pirates, they landed on the coast of Malayasia with the threat of tigers in the forest. They were taken to a refugee camp on an island off the coast of Malayasia, where they had to build their own shelter from trees growing on the mountain just inland. They ate canned beans provided by the United Nations. More and more boat people poured in. Water ran short. Thieves came in the pitch black night. The one redeeming feature was that the Ngos lived at the water's edge, and the children played daily in the crystal clear waters. They have wonderful memories of that. After a year delegates from various countries came to select among the refugees, if they could also find sponsors in those countries. The United States Catholic Conference was the sponsoring body that helped resettle many thousands of people in the United States. We welcomed them to our home in Cullman.

After all the trauma these thirteen people had been through, nerves were stretched thin and warfare went on within the family. When I saw evidence of this we moved the four teenage girls, Em Tien's unmarried sisters, to the floor where I lived in Joseph Hall. Sister Monica in her eighties became their great-grandma, Sister Maurus grandma, and I was Mom. Em and Minh were sent to Cullman High, while Buoi and Hon found jobs. They went through great suffering in adjusting to our life on this other side of the world. Everything was different—climate, language, food, customs. I saw the daily struggle they went through up close and personal acting as their mom, teaching English, helping with homework, listening to heavy hearts, and listening to the longings that all young girls have. I loved to watch their petit hands as they prepared a meal with total beauty and gracefulness. I was never able to talk with their aged parents because of the language barrier, but I deeply admired their goodness and graciousness as a family.

A major transformation within me during those years was the growth of maternal love. We have three widows in our Community who raised children, but ordinarily Sisters are not mothers. I had recognized early in religious life how selfish I could be. I could make my own little world revolve around me. I had earnestly prayed to be able to love. Now I felt a maternal love born within me. I grew to dearly love my girls, these "little women." They are the most marvelous gift God has ever given me. They remain a most important part of my life.

One day after the Ngos had lived with us for two years, I had an overwhelming interior experience. I stood in the backyard with Em Tien as he suffered over yet another major decision. He had been such a responsible Chinese oldest son, caring for his aged parents, his wife and five children, and his four youngest sisters. He tried to figure out what was best for his family, how to support them, how to make peace within his household. He thought it would be good to move to California where they had some other relatives. And, of course, there was always an underlying fear of the KKK when the Klansman got out of prison.

As I was listening to Em Tien's agony, I suddenly felt as if a veil were removed from my eyes. There before me stood the wounded, suffering Christ. My heart was deeply touched by his pain and struggle, his carrying of the cross of a divided family, of dislocation and relocation. An instant later, I felt as if I were the Christ. Wondrous love flowed out of my heart for the suffering man before me. It all happened in a moment. Em Tien never knew. But it was a transforming moment for me. I weep as I recall it. It was a tiny window into the real world, the world that is total love, with all in God. All human suffering enfolded in God's tender love. I can never forget it.

In the years to come, I would learn the Catholic Social Principles from the best minds in the United States and I would teach these principles repeatedly in the churches of Alabama. The basic foundational principle from which the teaching is built is that we are made in the image and likeness of God. Each person represents Christ. Looking at another human being is as close as we can get to looking directly at God. To say it in the negative, to lay hands violently on another human being is the closest we can come to laying hands violently on God. Our path is to see Christ in another, to honor Christ in another, to be Christ for one another. On that day in the backyard, I received a direct deep knowing of this reality. It is ever fresh in my mind.

The first week the Ngo family was in Cullman, I asked them a typical southern question in making a new acquaintance, "What church do you go to?" Em Tien, the only one who spoke any English told me they were Confucian. I knew this was more of a moral way of life than a religion with prayer and ritual. But as I got to know the family better, I saw the aged parents pray for a long time each morning, Grandpa reading his scripture, Grandma praying with her mala (rosary). I would see them celebrate their feast days as a family with prayer and incense and eating special foods. I came to understand that the Ngos were Chinese Buddhists, with the wonderful goddess of compassion Quan Yin as an important part of their devotional life. But on that first Sunday the family was in Cullman I invited them to Mass, telling them they may like to see what most Americans do every Sunday. Henceforth every Sunday morning all thirteen people lined up in the back pew of Sacred Heart Monastery chapel. I told them they did not have to come to please us. But they smiled and said, "Our father (the old man) says it is very peaceful here."

It was many years before I was able to share in their religious expression. It was a mystical experience for me. More years had passed. Buoi, the eldest of the four little women, had married and moved to Houston with her husband, Son. Minh, the youngest of the four, and I went to visit her there. Buoi was so excited that we had come at that time because the new temple has just been opened for the Chinese from Vietnam, the Temple of the God of all gods. She wanted to take us. It was the feast of the Birth of Heaven and Earth. This Buddhist feast comes at their New Year, the biggest feast of the year.

We arrived at what looked like a rather ordinary house in a residential area, but it had a big red oriental gate at the street. Passing through the gate, in the middle of the path we saw a banquet table with a roasted pig and an array of fruits and foods they had loved in Vietnam. As we continued on and entered the building we faced an altar with a three-foot statue of the "God of all gods" surrounded by candles and incense. Around the walls of the room were other altars with large statues. Incense wafted through the air.

There was a lot of activity going on. People were chanting and praying at various altars. Children were running about, helping with little things. Someone was gonging the big gong on the right side. Little bells were tinkling. Buoi, as a very proper Chinese woman, began her rituals. She had brought with her incense and fruit to put on each altar. Before each altar she carefully placed four pieces of fruit on a plate and presented that. Then lit incense and knelt to pray. Holding the incense between her folded fingers she bowed and prayed.

Meanwhile Minh was walking around with me telling me about everything, stories of the various gods and goddesses and what devotional things people were doing before the altars. She said, "See, Sister Mary, this is how we pray. At the Catholic church everyone comes together at one time and they all sing or pray the same thing. At our temple we each say our own prayers."

I asked various theological questions, but got only a gentle laugh, "We just do it this way. We do not think about why we do it this way."

Then a man in robes followed by two robed women began walking together to each altar chanting. I asked if he were a priest, and was told that he was. I said, "The women can't be nuns because they wear makeup and jewelry."

"You are right," Minh said, "My Mother did this in Vietnam. She helped the priest at our temple."

Within moments the priest called out and all the people in the temple formed a single circle around the entire room. They moved prayerfully around in the circle, chanting together. I happened to be standing just behind the altar of the "God of all gods", so it placed me in the center of the circle. I looked at all those very ordinary praying people, the very old and the youngest children, and thought of all they had been through—the years of war, the terrors, the flight, the time in the refugee camps, the hard readjustment to another land. Here they were praying with deep faith and in the most heartfelt way, singing God's praises and asking for mercy. I was touched most deeply. As the chanting and the circling continued, I felt a great rising of energy in the whole room as the Presence of the Divine covered her people in love. Suddenly the priest gave a call and everyone dispersed. The energy whooshed through me. I stood in awe.

Moments later the priest came up and welcomed me and asked if I had had anything to eat. When I said no, he went to the steam table of food to the left of the entrance door, but it was empty. So he told some of the children to take food off the altars to bring to me. I know I had communion that day. And it was most glorious!

REFLECTION

Where have you seen the face of Christ in another? Describe your experience.

Have you experienced the religious ritual of another world religion? Describe.

Clockwise from top:
1. McGehee family portrait, St. Louis, 1946: John, Mary, Alfreda (mother), Hiram (father)
2. Mary and John at their clubhouse built on sandbox
3. McGehee sibling portrait, Tuscaloosa, 1952: Rose, Mary and John
4. Mary dressed as Dominican Sister for Kindergarten play: *"I could memorize all the lines."*

Clockwise from top left:
1. Bride of Christ, June 14, 1961: Mary about to receive the habit
2. 1963: Sister Mary in front of monastery chapel
3. Final Vows, June 15, 1967: Anna Kohake Meyer (Grandmother), Sister Mary, Alfreda Meyer McGehee (Mother)
4. Sacred Heart Monastery Chapel, Cullman, AL
5. The Gropers, 1973-1974: Sisters Renee, Felice, Edwina, Karen, Mary and Yvette
6. Spring 1980: Sisters Maurus Allen and Mary

Clockwise from top:

1. Sister Mary and the Ngo family, printed in the Cullman Times August 12, 1979: top: Em, Chang, Minh, Buoi, Hon, Em Tien, Payee, Thanh. bottom. Sister Mary, May, Phung, Duc, Ngoc, Van

2. Sister Mary and Chinese friends: Judy Chan, Elizabeth Wu, Yen Vuong

3. Death Row, December 23, 1991, Altmore, AL: James Cochran, Shirley Nolan, Arthur Giles, Sister Mary

4. Yoga class, October 1982: printed in the Decatur Daily

Clockwise from top left:
1. Sister Mary, 1996: Photo by Melissa Springer - used in "A Tribe of Warrior Women, Breast Cancer Survivors", Published by Crane Hill in 1996.
2. Sister Mary - Massage Therapist
3. Centering Prayer Leaders, February 14, 1999 in Birmingham, AL: Aloysius Golden, Sandra Lawler, Sister Mary McGehee, Caroline Humphreys, Deana Tschache, Thomas Keating OCSO, Danette and Mike Burkhalter, Karen Pilman
4. Mother's 60th Wedding Anniversary, June 15, 1997: John, Alfreda, Rose and Sister Mary

Chapter 10: JUSTICE

After the experience of the Klan threatening the Ngo family and because of it, Sister Anne and I went to a meeting in Atlanta about the resurgence of the Ku Klux Klan that was happening across America in the early 1980s. Here for the first time I heard Civil Rights leaders and their message of Gospel love and their call for unity of all in Christ. I had been asleep to their theology during the 1960s. 1963 was the first year I taught school. I was in Birmingham when the 16th Street Baptist Church was bombed. We heard about that bombing and the assassination of John F. Kennedy two months later from Huntley-Brinkley. In that decade we still lived a rather cloistered life and did not leave our own school or convent. That was our first year to be allowed to watch the evening news on television.

We had been ordered by Archbishop Toolen not to take part in any demonstrations. The great end of segregation did not touch my life directly, so I lived in relative unawareness. At that meeting in Atlanta, I heard the Civil Rights leaders theorize that there is an upsurge of the Klan every time there are hard times economically. Their analysis was that the rich supported the Klan in order to keep the workers divided. It was easy to do that racially in the South because of years of learned prejudice. Unions seldom took hold here because workers could not trust one another. I began to see the Klansmen in the courtroom with new eyes. I had heard that some in their families were unemployed and had even applied for work at Nicholson File only to be denied. And here were people arriving from Asia who got good jobs because they had influential friends. My eyes were opening, and my heart was beginning to grow in compassion.

The experience began my dialogue with African Americans. I had become a polite southern woman who would not ask direct questions. Now I asked direct questions about racism, and I got more than an earful. In the following years I would take part in numerous Undoing Racism and Prejudice Reduction workshops, which allowed me to hear personal stories about how prejudice and racism continues real suffering right around me. I helped begin dialogue sessions between predominantly black and white Catholic parishes in the Diocese. My heart was opening to suffering that had been surrounding me all my life, and I had never seen it so clearly.

Earlier in 1978 when I attended the Federation General Chapter in Denver, the entire discussion was on social justice. I intellectually saw a point to it, but I had a strong reaction against it being a priority for Benedictine women. If we were not staffing so many schools, were we just trying to find some other work to justify our existence, worker women that we were? I wanted renewal to be directed toward a more contemplative life style.

But a sea of social changes had happened and was happening, and I got swept on the tide. I began listening to stories of suffering people around the globe, and my soul was broken open. Compelling things were happening that grabbed me and thrust me forward. The 1980s became a decade of phenomenal, irreversible change for me. It happened step by step, but before I knew it I was taken by the tide.

In 1980 Benedictines around the world celebrated the 1500th birthday of St. Benedict in all kinds of ways. American Benedictine women founded Benedictines for Peace to reclaim the ancient motto, *Pax* (peace), that has hung over our doorways for centuries. In that time of the unprecedented growth of the nuclear arms race, we went to Washington, D.C., to pray and vigil all night for the U.S. bishops as they crafted their pastoral letter "The Challenge of Peace." In August 1985 five of us from Cullman returned to Washington to help tie the Ribbon of Peace around the Pentagon, joining fifteen miles of people in a celebration of hope.

As a Benedictine Community we began a serious pondering

of world issues and the Christian call to social justice. We formed a Peace and Justice Committee as one of our standing committees. Its purpose was to continue to educate us Sisters about Catholic social teaching and to keep us all apprised of important issues in our day. We developed a process for taking a corporate public stand when a situation compelled us to do so. We hosted the Gathering of the Catholic Committee of the South (CCS) that had been reorganized by the Glenmary Commission on Justice. At the CCS Gathering each November, a mixed array of a hundred or more people in the struggle spoke out. I listened attentively to blacks tell of blatant and violent racism, to coal miners of Kentucky tell of environmental devastation, cane workers of Louisiana tell of their unfair working conditions, migrant workers from Arkansas tell about their trek across the border, women without running water from Pine Apple, Alabama, Cherokees from North Carolina. I saw the beautiful connecting of so many races, religions, genders, and nations.

We Benedictines also alerted Alabamians along the railroad tracks to the white train carrying nuclear warheads, joined the Nuclear Freeze movement, and traveled to Kings Bay Trident Submarine Base in Georgia after each Christmas for the Feast of Holy Innocents. We hosted Salvadoran and Nicaraguan refugees and demonstrated at the School of the Americas in Fort Benning, Georgia. Some of us went to Mexico for a two-week immersion in the political and social realities of Latin America. I can still hear Julia Esquivel tell of torture and death of tens of thousands at the hands of the death squads in Guatemala, in the gripping way only a poet can, and Father David Rodriguez sing of Archbishop Romero as he prepared to return to El Salvador to face possible martyrdom himself.

Each pope for more than one hundred years has written strong encyclicals calling the world to stop all its horrible violence and terrible injustices. They developed a comprehensive moral teaching based on the dignity of each human person and the need for social structures to be created or reformed to protect the common good of all. They began to speak of God's preferential option for the poor. In 1971 the World Synod of Bishops wrote:

> "Listening to the cry of those who suffer violence and are oppressed by unjust systems and structures, and hearing the appeal of a world that by its perversity contradicts the plan of its Creator, we have shared our awareness of the Church's vocation to be present in the heart of the world by proclaiming the Good News to the poor, freedom to the oppressed, and joy to the afflicted.
>
> ...**Action on behalf of justice and participation in the transformation of the world** fully appear to us as a **constitutive dimension of the preaching of the Gospel**, or in other words, of the Church's mission for the redemption of the human race and its liberation from every oppressive situation."

In the Diocese of Birmingham, a Peace and Justice Commission was formed by committed leaders after the Call to Action gathering in 1976. Ultimately I became the Director of the Office of Peace and Justice in the Diocese of Birmingham. In 1982 Tom Brassington, Director of the Office of Religious Education, came to Cullman looking for someone to teach about social justice to teachers and catechists. Sisters Martina, Bertha, and I became a traveling road show to schools and parishes around north Alabama. I began serious reading of the church documents and studies of various worldwide injustices. Then I joined the Diocesan Peace and Justice Commission, and in 1985 became its first paid coordinator to begin an official office for the Diocese. Finally, as the Diocese began its fifth season of RENEW in 1987, I was made full- time Director in order to introduce Catholic social teaching to leaders of small faith communities in all the parishes. Subsequent to that appointment I visited each pastor in the Diocese to explain that Bishop Vath wished each parish to have a Social Concerns Committee as part of its official parish structure. This was actually received quite willingly, and I mentored those parish committees. There was also teaching of the Peace Pastoral of 1983 and a major project with the Pastoral on the Economy of 1986. Each winter I went to Washington, D.C., for the conference for Diocesan Social Action Directors and was briefed on the most current national and international issues, then visited our senators and representatives about these issues. One of my favorite events was the celebration of International Catholic Women we held twice, with colorful sharing of stories, song, dance, and food of most of the cultures living in Birmingham.

As a representative of the Diocese, I served on the Board of Greater Birmingham Ministries (GBM), and later Alabama Arise. It was the time of the closing of U.S. Steel and massive unemployment in Birmingham. Other businesses were going to part-time employment or no benefits, so there was also great underemployment. The number of homeless on the streets was growing. GBM began negotiations with the utility companies so the poor would not have their heat and electricity cut off. I met every Thursday for the brown bag lunch meeting with the Economic Justice group that analyzed all these issues. It was most important learning for me, and a wonderful experience of real collaboration of all the churches.

I found that my mode of ministry was now very different compared to my perfectionist days of the sixties. Then, I strove very hard to make things happen, so everything seemed a heavy job. Now, I worked continuously, but it seemed more in response to need, and I felt more centered.

What was happening to me interiorly, to my prayer? I did, of course, pray with my Sisters, whether I was at the monastery or with other Sisters with whom I stayed in the parishes, but I was on the road every week. I did take time for meditation and *lectio,* but often that got shortened. I did *lectio* with the stories I was hearing, with *the signs of the times.* At the suggestion of Ron DelBene, my spiritual director at the time, I got a small journal I could easily carry. Each night I recorded how I had seen the face of Christ that day. It helped to keep me attentive, to look for that face among all the people I encountered.

I read the very small books by Thich Nhat Hanh about mindfulness, and tried to be present to "each slice of the tangerine" of my day. When I felt the spirit of "rush," I would take slow mindful breaths and come back to myself, opening my eyes and acknowledging the gifted world I walked in. I slowed my pace so I could see.

The spirituality of nonviolence became very important to me. I read Gandhi, Dr. Martin Luther King Jr., Eugene Sharp, and Jim Douglass. It drew me profoundly. I remembered Brother David Steindl-Rast saying, "Who better than a monk to demonstrate publicly for peace."

As my workday extended with works of peace and justice, the prayer spaces dwindled. I took that in stride and felt I truly walked in the Presence. I was not so insistent about a certain form or structure of prayer but sought to listen from my heart wherever I was.

I had begun this decade wounded, decimated,
left nearly dead on the side of the road.
I crept and crawled around, moaned and groaned.
peering into other places looking for my ideal.
I laughed sadly at them all.
Nothing was true and pure goodness.
All was sham and wounded and broken in various ways.

I writhed more.
Is this what life is all about?
One great joke?
The dreams and deep urgings just there to be frustrated?
Then out of the side of my eye I saw others crawl forward

the Ngos stripped, beaten down, humiliated
the women of Mexico surviving, but just barely
the earth herself jolted and pricked and spit upon, almost blown
inside out
the people of Israel/Palestine divided and entrenched in hate, religion condoning
the Blacks of Alabama enslaved, bombed, raped or castrated,
lynched
the poor and homeless blamed for their illness, unemployment, and
confusion.

My arms stretch out and embrace them all.
My womb aches.
I try to listen to my body.
It no longer marches stridently toward any goal.
It sits and waits and rocks and feels the pain.
It knows the suffering Christ in so many faces and forms.

It would take a whole book to tell the adventures of those days. I was changed and transformed because of the people I met, the stories I heard, and the social inequities, life struggles and wonderful human spirit that I witnessed.

There is one story I would like to include here, about a friend on Death Row, to illustrate the strength of spirit I encountered.

In 1989 Alabama executed four men in quick succession, our first executions since the Supreme Court declared most states' execution laws unconstitutional in 1976. I found myself standing before the Jefferson County Court House with my counterparts from other denominations and service organizations. At night we saw the TV stations use us as part of the media show, juxtaposed against the "fry'em" demonstrators at the prison in Atmore. We realized we needed a better strategy to change public opinion about the death penalty. A diverse group formed the Alabama Committee to Abolish the Death Penalty. Shortly, some prisoners from Atmore contacted us to say, "How can you speak for us if you do not know us?" Excellent point. These prisoners had formed Project Hope, also to work toward ending state execution. Three of us went on a hot August day to meet four of their leaders: Jesse Morrison, Gary Brown, Brian Baldwin, and Bo Cochran. I was very impressed by this racially mixed group of men and the respect they had for one another. We continued to meet with Project Hope leaders each August. It is Bo I wish to tell you about.

Some years after I met him the first time and after nineteen years on death row, James "Bo" Cochran's appeals got to the federal level. He was given a new trial because he had not been tried initially by a jury of his peers—eleven jurors were white and only one was black. Bo was black. He was brought to the Birmingham jail to await trial, and I went to visit him there. During the visit Bo began telling me about all the gang kids housed in the jail and how they came to him for grandfatherly advice. As he talked, I kept looking at him through the bars and realized that Bo's dark face was glowing.

I was amazed and asked, "How are you, Bo? Your trial is next week. How are you coping?"

He responded, "I am really fine. I do not know what will happen next week. But it doesn't matter what happens in that courtroom. If I am found guilty and am given life imprisonment, that's okay because I have been there. If they find me guilty and give me death, that is okay because I know where I am going. If they find me innocent and set me free, that would be wonderful. But it really does not matter what happens. I am fine."

My mouth dropped open. I had listened to many retreatants who came to Sacred Heart, and I doubted that I had ever been told that *whatever* happened to them would be okay. I remembered that Bo had already been in prison for nineteen years, and asked, "How did you get this way?"

He answered, "Well, when I first got to prison I was mean and hateful. I hated everybody. I gave the guards a hard time. Gradually I realized the guards were just doing their jobs. They did not dislike me. I had to face myself and admit that I was mean and hateful really because I hated my Daddy, who was a steel worker. He had abused me as a kid. Once I admitted my hate for my Daddy, I had another decision to make. I made the decision to turn my life over to Jesus. Now, that wasn't easy. It took me a long time. But I have given my life to Jesus, and let go of hate. So whatever happens, that is okay. I'm in His hands."

I was stunned. I wanted to say, "Never have I seen such great faith in all of Alabama." I knew I was looking at a truly developed human being, a saint. I also knew that our society would rather not have to see Bo and the others on death row. We place them out of sight and imagine them totally evil, like rats that we want to exterminate.

At Bo's trial he was found guilty of armed robbery but not murder. He was released from prison the following week since he had served his time. Some weeks later when I was back at the prison, as I was being searched before entering, I asked the guard if she had heard that Bo Cochran was found "not guilty" and was out of prison.

She jumped up and down and got very excited. "I am so glad," she exclaimed, "He is one of the nicest men I have ever met!"

Today Bo lives in East Lake in Birmingham, working and happily married to Shirley Nolan, doing extra service for his neighbors because he was unable to do that for so many years.

Brian Baldwin was executed in 1999. Gary Brown was executed in 2002. Jesse Morrison's sentence was commuted to life without parole. The State of Alabama stopped using the electric chair, but it still executes by lethal injection, considering it a more humane method to terminate someone's life. Since 1989 by the time of this writing, Alabama has executed twenty-seven people, among them were ones who had dementia, bipolar disorder, severe retardation, severe mental illness, and one Vietnam veteran. Only a handful of countries continues to use execution as punishment. Most of them are very repressive governments.

REFLECTION

Following are some questions the Peace and Justice Commission of the Diocese of Birmingham in Alabama sent out in 1991 when it led a process of reflection on the Alabama Bishops' pastoral letter on economic justice "Make Justice Your Aim."

Have you ever been poor? If so, what effect did that experience have on you?

Has anyone in your family ever been poor? Have any of your friends, neighbors or co-workers ever been deprived of the basic necessities for life? If so, briefly describe. What impact did that have on the family?

Have you ever worked as a volunteer with people who were poor: If so, how did that experience make you feel? What impact did it have on you?

My added questions:
In what ways has your social consciousness evolved? How did this happen?

What do you do in your daily busy life to stay mindful of the presence of God?

Chapter 11: YEAR OF JUBILEE

In my fiftieth year I realized I was in the year of Jubilee. I began reading everything I could find on the topic. It seems that it goes this way:

God made the world in six days. On the seventh day He/She sat back, took a deep breath, looked around, and said, "This is good. This is really good!" So we are invited, in fact commanded, to do the same thing. For six days we roll up our sleeves and do all sorts of creative things that need doing. But on the seventh day (or in some proportion of one to six) we sit back, take a really deep breath, and open our eyes to see how great and good everything is. We see all that *God* has done within us and around us.

There are two parts to this commandment about the Sabbath. The first part is all the "do nots." Do not cook. Do not clean. Do not light a fire. Do not walk too many steps. Do not go to market. Do not put a burden on your ox, your ass, your servant or slave, or yourself. *Do not do! Stop!* Enjoy a deep breath. Then take some really good rest. Why? Because you need it. But even more importantly, otherwise you might think that *you* do it all. You may start thinking that you are God.

The second part is "to delight." Open your eyes and actually look at the beauties that surround you. Savor things slowly. Notice with all your senses what is all around you, and open your heart to delight. Enjoy your spouse and your children. Read the scriptures. Do everything playfully. Sing and dance. Why? Because everything is a gift. It is meant to be enjoyed. What if we walk by it all and do not see or enjoy, and end up never being grateful? But if we are grateful, the gift will return us to the Giver. Then we will overflow with thankfulness for all our blessings. We will adore our Creator.

Well, if this is the Sabbath day, the sabbatical year is a year-long rest and celebration. Of course, the big question is, "How do we survive?" And the answer is, "Trust. God is God and will provide."

The Jubilee Year is the seven times seventh year, the forty-ninth or the fiftieth year. It is the super special rest-and-delight-all-year-long year. But it is even more. It is the time for all of society to be reorganized as if we are returning to the beginning, everything set up in God's way. Slaves and indentured servants are freed. If land has been amassed by one family but others have none, the land is redistributed so all have their fair share, so all can have their basic life needs met. Land is to lie fallow so nutrients can be restored. And, of course, all workers have free time. It is a year to rest, to enjoy and delight. Why? So we don't forget that God really, really is in charge. And God wants us to be godly too, and to love and share with others as much as He/She does.

If this is Jubilee, I thought, I pondered what it would look like in my life. I wrote up a page using the images of Jubilee and applied them to the inner journey. I immediately noticed some things about myself. First, I realized I had always been unrelentingly hard on myself, had enslaved myself, so I decided to "Lighten up, Honey." I did not push myself so much. I purposely planned fun events on my calendar: concerts, plays, movies, evenings with friends. And I asked for a 30-day retreat. This one was to be a second honeymoon with God. I needed to just rest and enjoy. I did not need any disciplined Zen meditation or Jesuit strictness. I needed time in nature to bask in my Beloved's love. So, I asked my friend, Notre Dame Sister Catherine Griffiths, for space with the Notre Dame Sisters in Ipswich, Massachusetts.

It was a most glorious month! God blessed me so wondrously. I slept as late as I could each morning. If I woke up and felt crotchety, I turned over and put myself back to bed. The sun each day seemed brighter than the day before. I took long walks through the woods or down to the shore. I savored the taste of my food, felt the wind on my skin and blow through my hair, and smelled the earthy forest fragrances. It couldn't have been more delight-full. I shared with Catherine a couple times a week and took some outings with her. She gave me Macrina Wiederkehr's wonderful booklet that was a tool to help ponder each stage of one's life, spaced over the Lenten season.

The biggest sense that arose within me was overwhelming gratitude for every stage, every aspect of my life. Just overwhelming gratitude. God had poured one blessing after another upon me for the whole of my life. Before, I tended to jerk myself by my shirt front and say, "Be grateful." But I was rushing around being responsible for galoshes all over the place. Now, I had space and time to become aware, to allow myself to be opened in gratitude.

The negative I got in touch with was resentment, deep anger that I held onto and continued to feed. I realized I walked around with lots of resentments about one thing or another. The biggest were directed toward some of my past Prioresses. I could now see that this was really ridiculous. Here I was holding on to this ancient anger burning a hole in me, fuming away. But it was all in the past. So, I decided to try to dismantle this stuff. I knew that would not be easy, that it would be a process.

Sometime in midway in my Jubilee retreat, Catherine told me about some local chiropractors who did all kinds of holistic healing. I had felt a lump in my breast months earlier and had been to the doctor who had told me to wait for my regular mammogram, guessing that it was a cyst. But I thought maybe these women could do something, so I went. They started by saying, "Our theory is that whatever is going on in your body is 1% physical, 9% mental, and 90% spiritual. Our theory is that a cyst is walled off waste matter. What waste are you holding onto? Our theory is that the right side of the body is the father or masculine, and the left side is the mother or feminine. So what is your problem with your mother?"

I thought, "Wow! How did they know? Yes, this resentment has been waste matter that I have clung to for years, too many years! Mothers, not Mother. I am angry at some of my Sisters." The experience was an affirmation through my body of what I was uncovering in my spiritual searching. So I ended the retreat saying, "Hi, I'm Mary. I am a resenter. I am beginning a recovery program."

REFLECTION

Ponder your own individual need for Jubilee. Look at parts of yourself that can be affected by the year of Jubilee:

I am the farmer. I give rest to the land of
my inner self—no planting, pruning,
or harvesting. In what ways can I rest deeply?
Can I rest from criticizing myself for any deficiencies,
imperfections, or past sins?
Do I trust enough that God really cares for me and is the
One who is in charge of growing me? Who is in charge
here anyway?
I stop to see what God has done in my life—and list the
delights.
I savor what is good.
I remember all God's actions to save me in the past and in
the present.

I am the earth. I have given fruit and yield of all kinds.
Now I rest and just soak in the spring rain and let the miracles of growth spring from within me. I am gentle with
myself.
What innate gifts/talents do I discover about myself?
What gives me energy?

I am the slave.
What do I need to be freed from?
Drives and compulsions?

Reflection

What binds me? Perhaps fear or resentments or life's disappointments?

What have I served long enough (six years…forty-nine years) and now need to be released from?

How do I feel when I am freed?

I am the buyer of the land. Now I will return the land to the original owners so they and their children may have their needs met.

Is there anything in my life that is out of proportion that needs adjusting according to God's ways?

I am the banker. On Jubilee I will cancel all debts with no payments given back to me. With whom do I need to reconcile?

What grudges/resentments need to be cancelled with no satisfaction paid back to me?

Can I forgive as Jesus does?

Can I give freely with no strings attached?

I am the debtor. How do I feel with my debt pardoned?

Can I let go of any ill feelings I have held onto? How will I give thanks?

I am the Jubilee celebrator. What gives me life that I can choose more dramatically?

For what am I grateful? What do I celebrate?

What do I want to sing about? To dance about?

82

Chapter 12: BODY AND SOUL

During the month of my fiftieth birthday, I had my regular mammogram and found out I had breast cancer. "Yes, indeed," I thought, "This resentment stuff is cancerous! But I have already made a choice to release it. I have already begun a recovery process."

I had a mastectomy. It was not easy, but amazing things happened. Somehow for me it felt like I was thoroughly attending to my resentments. I allowed the "cutting out" to represent the resentments being removed. The cancer treatment gave me extended time for healing and renewal. It became part of the next wondrous transition in my life.

My surgery and chemotherapy were certainly life changing. As I prepared for the mastectomy I suddenly realized I had already passed through the prime of my life. I had not even known it and reveled in it. Now I was on an irreversible downward slope. I also realized I had never really thanked my body for its wonder and perfection. I wept for loosing such perfect balance and harmony. In yoga I had always felt so good as I bent and arched, so agile and limber. I loved twisting in the yoga postures and feeling the energy and centeredness of my body. It had always been a good nest for my soul. It was a marvelous temple of God. Now a part was to be chopped off and other parts weakened. I read that irreversible damage would be done to my arm when the lymph nodes were all removed. I grieved. I could hear the Queen in Alice in Wonderland cry, "Off with her breast! Off with her breast!" Some arbitrary authority seemed ready to maim me.

It was extremely hard to make each decision about my options in rapid succession: Can I admit I have cancer? How bad is it? Should I consent to a mastectomy and an axillary dissection? Should I have reconstruction? If so, should it be an implant under the breast muscle? Or reconstruction from the rectus abdominis? I had a weekend to think about it. My whole body cried out: "No unnecessary invasion!" I decided I could not put my muscles and body through any more than was necessary. It was enough to have a breast taken, my left arm weakened, and to know that I lived with cancer—all irreversible life changes. "What is is!" I thought.

I took music I loved to the hospital with me. I could tell the nurses enjoyed coming into my room. I felt surrounded by loving, healing energy as many friends visited and sent notes. I was overwhelmingly blessed and supported by the Communion of Saints. Unfortunately we less often receive such concern when we have mental suffering or are sick in the heart or soul. With a physical illness, the care is wondrous. I graciously received all the care and concern expressed for me.

I had many more emotional ups and down as I went through six months of chemotherapy. Initially I had an especially hard time thinking of killing chemicals entering my body. Then a friend gave me a "pac man" visualization. I imagined the seven dwarfs with their picks and shovels going in with the drugs. I sang with them, "Hi ho, hi ho, it's off to work we go…" I imagined them carrying away all the cancer cells. Yet there were many up days and down days. During those months I often wrote in my journal that I was not myself.

One helpful art practice during this healing time was to draw mandalas. A mandala is a circle with a centerpoint, usually about the size of a dinner plate, the size of one's head. Essentially it is an image of one's self. Many of my mandalas had pink, fuchsia, mauve, and purple tones. *Creating Mandalas* by Susanne Fincher suggested that those colors were about physical healing. It felt true to me.

I had two very significant dreams during those months. In the first dream I walked through a bright airy room, passing things of the past—a crying child, books, a prayer group with candles and

84

a picture of the four women martyrs of El Salvador who died December 2, 1980, but in my dream a placard said December 3. Then I exited the building and went down a path with a handrail on the right. To the left were beautiful deeply colored mountains, a strikingly gorgeous scene of strong green, purple, and blue—no fog, just sun-bright color. I was awed by the beauty before me as I glided down the mountainside guided by the handrail on my right. I passed one especially vivid scene of mountain passes and wished I could linger to soak in the beauty, but I was moving fast. I looked down and saw the stairs going down infinitely, like a dangling string. I was not afraid, but I screamed because of the shock of the depth. Someone touched me on my shoulder, and I realized there were lots of people around me. We turned and walked into the night.

The dream awed me with the deep inner world—vivid, deeply colored, beautiful. I was told to leave the things of the past—hurts and causes. It was not yet time to go down to the infinite totally, but the invitation came to go deeper and see and be awed, to be overwhelmed by the beauty. The dream touched me deeply and was a wondrous beckoning symbol during the difficult days of recovery. It was an image of the infinite inner world of my soul.

The second dream came after I had started chemotherapy. It was a strong dream of torture, dark and cold. I awoke haunted by the dream, knowing I was actually being tortured: breast whacked off, whittled out in my arm pit, injected with chemicals giving unpleasant side effects. I felt awful. All the emotions surfaced.

With that image imprinted strongly on my awareness, I walked out of my residence, Joseph Hall, that Saturday morning to go down the hill to work with a retreat group. In the valley before me lay the very real devastation of a tornado that had hit us the month before. More than twenty giant oak and hickory trees were lying roots up, twisted and tangled before me. Suddenly, in instant replay from my memory bank, came scenes of the last ten years. They were scenes in which I was face-to-face with bodily harm. Breast cancer, surgery, and chemotherapy had brought me the visceral knowing of dismemberment and destruction. When I had experienced the other events, part of me denied the horror that I now remembered. I became hysterical. I stayed in that hysteria with many tears, a state I am definitely not prone to, for most of the day.

What I remembered was driving in the dark of night to respond to a KKK bomb threat on refugees, the vast destruction of a tornado that took more than two years to clean up, traveling all over north Alabama in a diocesan car that broke down repeatedly and unexpectedly, being shouted at for reporting on a friend's peace journey to Iraq just before the bombing of war started, the silence of the hierarchy during the first war in Iraq where more than 10,000 were killed, including children, mothers, and grandmothers.

As I mulled about my vision, I realized that each of these flashbacks was a life-and-death situation, not an ordinary day in Mary's life. I was astounded by my depth of emotion. I was astonished that I had not reacted before. Secondly, I realized that each flashing scene involved men of my church, men near whom I lived or with whom I worked. In each case they had disregarded me and other women as we were left to face grave danger alone. As each event happened, my mode was to handle what needed to be handled, to rise above the negative and do something constructive. Now I was filled with deep hurt and anger at these men because I had been ignored, laughed at or shouted at, and then abandoned to face possible death. Why had I endured such disregard and disdain in silence? I was a human being. I was working hard in the church. I did matter!

These specific situations did not summarize all that these men were as persons, but I was deeply hurt by their lack of regard at these extreme times. I had on occasion suffered lesser indignities from them, but these were about life and death. If they had no better response as I and others faced grave danger, could I trust them as brothers and fathers of my church? Would they be sensitive to my ordinary concerns if they had no regard in these situations? What was I suppose to do? Was it my place to open their eyes, if they could not even notice or care when lives were threatened? After such abusive behavior did I need to carry their galoshes too? All I knew to do was to present this wound in my heart to the Divine Healer.

******

Many friends offered various alternative therapies as I recovered from breast cancer: therapeutic massage, healing touch, physical therapy, Feldenkrais, Reiki, polarity therapy, etc. It was wonderful to be touched and held and prayed over.

I began wondering if I could learn some of this and offer it to others at our retreat center. I knew I did not want to go to a massage school for a whole year. I did not want to spend that kind of time and money. Actually I wondered if I would be able to give massage therapy after dealing with cancer, and I wondered if I would like doing it. So I looked around the country and found that schools in California were more competitive and offered training in shortened formats. I went to Mueller College of Holistic Studies in San Diego. Through an intensive format, in ten days for ten hours a day I learned to give a basic one-hour massage.

I came home and gave massage. It was exactly a year after surgery that I opened my office for spiritual direction with massage and healing touch. In my wildest imagination I would never have pictured myself doing that kind of hands-on work. But it was wonderful! It was a marvelous way for me to stay really present, wondrously open to the Mystery. My directees liked my massage. I was able to do it and enjoyed doing it.

A year after my initial training I went back to San Diego for four more courses given within six weeks in the intensive format. Mueller College let me take the required academic courses at a junior college near Cullman. When the State of Alabama began licensing for massage therapy, I was ready to be one of the first people licensed.

At the same time the Holistic Nurses Association brought weekend *Healing Touch* courses to our retreat center. The energy work totally fascinated me, and I continued through the program and became a Certified Healing Touch Practitioner.

I have to admit that the energy picture I saw of myself was not a pretty sight. In *Healing Touch* by Hover-Kramer et al, I saw a diagram of a person with a Type A personality. I had to relate. The earth energy was closed off, the solar plexus overactive, and the person lived in the head. My usual mode was to work extremely hard and get totally worn out—very mental and very responsible. Galoshes again! I desired to be released, to just walk in the Presence of God on this beautiful green earth in the spirit of joy and gratitude. I desired to wake up to my own temple-ness, my own blessedness, my own divinity. This gift was given to me as I offered bodywork to others.

Working with the body made me ponder deeply the meaning of the Incarnation. God, the All Holy One, came into our fleshly existence, took it all on. He/She could have saved us in a flash, but instead came to be one of us, like us in all things. His/Her will is for us to be embodied, to enjoy this embodiment, to accept the full human reality in which we live, to revel in it, through life and into death. St. Paul calls the body the Temple of the Holy Spirit. My ministry became one of anointing those very living temples of the Living God.

Once when a retreatant came pondering how to articulate her ministry, I looked at my own as it was developing in those new ways. I realized two things: I was offering intercessory prayer, and I was there as a witness of awesome God-love. At an earlier stage I had questioned intercessory prayer. I wondered why I needed to remind God about another person. God knew that person so totally and loved her infinitely more than I could ever imagine. Yet I was experiencing this new work like intercessory prayer. For some mysterious reason God needed me to be in prayer for this person and to lovingly hold her, to complete a circle of love. I also saw my role was one of witness. To truly see, to marvel, to proclaim the saving action of our God as the marvels unfolded in the lives and bodies before me. Many levels of healing happened to people who came, and I had the unique opportunity to listen deeply. As I continue to stand in that circle of Divine Love, I witness the wonderful things God is doing within many souls and bodies. What a gift to all!

I would have told you I was not a feely-touchy kind of person. But God knew better. These modalities have been wonderful ways to listen deeply and to help others listen. They have been a most helpful aid to my ministry of spiritual direction. Its gift to me is the sense of Presence it brings. Most of my former ministries were of an administrative or organizational nature. With massage therapy and healing touch I am totally present, right there as my hands work with the tissues of the body or the energy field of the person. There is no past or future, only what the present holds and reveals. The whole experience is totally God-moment.

REFLECTION
Dialogue with the Body, as suggested in
Ira Progoff's works:

1. Name the weakest or most injured part
   of your body.
   Focus on it and become even more aware of it.
   Jot down words that come to you from this awareness.

2. What is the history of that part of your body?
   List anything that has happened to that part of your body during your lifetime.

3. Have a conversation with that part of your body.
   What does it want to say to you?
   What do you want to say to it?
   Continue to dialogue.

Dreamwork:
   Have you had any strong dreams that have special
   significance for you? Describe.
   Perhaps you would like to do some art work with them.

Chapter 13: **CENTERING**

My service in the Diocesan Peace and Justice Office ended with the first Gulf War. The Bishop and I had very different perspectives on the war, so I knew I could no longer be his spokesperson. I tried for a while to find a ministry in another social justice organization, but none was available, so I became more available for retreatants who come in a steady stream to Sacred Heart. I had been part of the team that started the Benedictine Spirituality and Conference Center in 1976, and over the years it had grown and developed more spirituality programs.

In 1991 as those last days of service in the Peace and Justice Office were winding down, Father Andy Kennedy came and asked if I would help teach Centering Prayer in the diocese. I had been meditating with the Zen method since the mid-1970s. In 1987 I had attended a ten-day workshop for Benedictines given in St. Joseph, Minnesota, by Father Thomas Keating, OCSO. So I knew the prayer and its effects. I was happy to share it with others.

I joined a stalwart group of men and women who met for twenty-four weeks in the Cathedral basement to pray this prayer, to watch an hour-long videotape each week of Father Thomas Keating, and to discuss the content. The video series, titled "The Spiritual Journey," was one of the best courses I had ever seen to explain the psychological effects of the contemplative prayer practice. Father Thomas, a Trappist, was the founder of Contemplative Outreach, Ltd. That organization, which is primarily a lay organization, is now international.

I joined the Contemplative Outreach Birmingham Steering Committee with Father Andy Kennedy and Judge Aloysius Golden and others. In time I became the Coordinator. Caroline Humphreys offered her secretarial skills. We began offering introductory workshops to any parish interested, had a national speaker each winter, and gave weekend retreats and a ten-day Intensive in Cullman at our retreat center.

Essentially Centering Prayer is a prayer of intention. One has the intention to be fully in God's presence. Of course, none of us is ever out of God's presence. We just forget that fact. During Centering Prayer one has the intention to say "yes" to God's action in one's life. Our minds wander, but when that happens we gently return to the "sacred word" that represents this heartfelt intention. To sit with this intention each morning and evening for an extended time allows God to draw us deeper and deeper into union, beyond our ego, beyond our "programs for happiness." It is a twenty-minute period to exercise our will to consent to God's love. If we can keep that up for twenty minutes twice a day, maybe we can continue to consent to God's will throughout our day. We so often stray, with our consciousness pulled here and there, our hearts divided, our lives fragmented with a frenetic pace and the intrusion of every kind of communication device. To be drawn into the silence and to practice directing our will to God alone each morning and evening will gradually allow God to transform us in the wondrous ways She wishes.

Just to sit, to be still, to linger in the Presence. Not to expect anything. Not to give God orders. Not to look for a message or an experience. But to trust our living God. To wait as Mary, with pregnancy. To let go of expectation. Of course, it means that whoever is daft enough to do this every day twice a day must have known an invitation at a deep level. Maybe an inner cry or craving for more. A sweet delight in a God-felt moment. But that was mere enticement.

It is risky business, this dealing with the Living God who was not planning to leave us alone anyway. I found it full of surprises.

With my great longing for a renewed monasticism I found myself sitting in circles of the most unlikely "monks." People of all ages, of all denominations, or none. People willing to risk losing friends when they dared to choose this relationship and this discipline. I realized that this prayer form allowed each person to free the monk within, to develop the part of herself that sought silence and solitude, and to stand alone before God, to let go of all but God. I delighted in God's surprise monasticism.

I saw a new ecumenism around me. Wherever we held workshops, the gathering was ecumenical. It was God's doing, not our planning. Folks arrived with a neighbor, a cousin, a friend. No one was denied who hungered for the simplicity of quieting to the raging world and of being still in the silence of Mystery. There was nothing to divide us. Just sit. Practice the intention to consent to God's presence and action. What might be God's action within and among us, but to make us sisters and brothers to one another?

As I began offering Healing Touch during this same period, I realized the one thing that made all the difference to the client was my own inner state. The more I could truly be in the Presence of the All Holy One, without my mind pulled in twenty or more other directions, the better for the one seeking healing. The more I consented to God's action, not my agenda, the more surprises and healings happened to bodies and souls. No expectations. No demands. Just to be open to the love and graciousness of our God.

I have now spent the past dozen years teaching Centering Prayer and Lectio Divina, while serving as Coordinator of Contemplative Outreach Birmingham. During that time I was also on the Team of the Benedictine Sisters' Retreat Center. So I gave countless workshops on prayer and various aspects of Catholic and Benedictine spirituality. Spirituality and prayer have become very popular. With all the sensual input and frenetic activity of postmodern life, people are seeking for their souls.

What is prayer? I share with you some of my ponderings:

Prayer is plowing the ground of ourselves because we are hardened—so we can receive the seed as it is cast by the Sower.

Prayer is quieting the mind lest we be unable to hear the Word when spoken—because of our infernal mind chatter.

Prayer is gentling the heart lest it be too hard and judgmental to recognize the Lover who beckons or appears.

Prayer is waiting until we are able to wake up to what IS. It is to receive the incarnation in all its fullness.

Prayer is being with the emotions as they soar and peak, rage and weep, until we know their lessons more truly.

Prayer is none of those things because we are incapable of doing any of them very well. It is being utterly loved by God. And at least getting some inkling of that. Or no inkling at all.

Prayer is waiting. It is nine months of pregnancy. It is care for a child. It is the lingering deterioration of the elderly. It is waiting for the soul.

Sometimes the reservoir has been damaged, and a hole appears where all life seems to rush out—by busy-ness, frenetic activity, cell phones, computers, entertainment, and other distractions. Sit by it. Have a no-goal prayer.

There are stuck times when the reservoir seems empty. One shouldn't try to force movement, but to let the waters of God's love seep in gradually and be restored. Gentle the self—walk in nature, rest a lot, do nurturing things. When a seed is in a rut, it digs deeper.

When I was a child, would God have preferred that I swing from the trapeze by my knees and build clubhouses on my sandbox, or visit the silent church and go to Mass?

We want union with God. Whose god? Do we want the American dream here too of a God experience? Perhaps this Camelot of our dreams is only to be glimpsed once or twice in our lives, else how could we have the longing in our hearts for more? For the Kingdom of God? For the Beloved Community? It is our Loving God who is bringing all into being. If we just consent. Cast yourself into the arms of the Living God.

REFLECTION
Sit or assume your most comfortable position.
Close your eyes.
Breathe deeply and comfortably.

Direct your intention to the Divine Presence dwelling within you.
Embrace God with faith and love.
Lovingly give yourself to God.

Let a single sacred word—perhaps the name of Jesus or Abba—
fall gently in your awareness, symbolizing your consent to God's
presence and loving action within you. Repeat it as often as may
be needed when you sense your mind following thoughts or
reflections elsewhere.

If you become aware of engaging with any other thoughts or feelings or bodily sensations, very gently return to the sacred word,
the symbol of your consent to God's love.

After approximately twenty minutes, slowly recite an affirmation,
or linger in the silence.

Chapter 14: MY BROTHER JOHN

When I look back to our childhood I have great admiration for our parents. John, the eldest, was born with the cord wrapped around his neck, so he was brain damaged. Mother and Daddy never treated him differently or showed any disappointment in him. They did spend a great deal of time and effort to train John with all the needed life skills. This they did very thoroughly. They also encouraged his creative and adventuresome nature throughout his life. As an adult he functioned about like a ten-year-old. One that age is able to do a lot, but abstract thinking is limited.

John was very gregarious. He had loyal best friends throughout his life in whatever city he lived: David Paridy in St. Louis, Tommy Lee with scouting in Tuscaloosa, Gene, Bob and Ray as adult friends in Alexandria, Virginia. John had a refreshing but disarming manner of saying directly whatever was on his mind. In fact, whatever was on his mind came right out of his mouth. All of it. He had an extremely annoying habit of talking incessantly, telling all the details whether one wanted them or not.

John and I were very close during all of childhood. I remember building two clubhouses together. The first was built up from our sandbox—uprights nailed to it, then orange crate slats nailed across from upright to upright. I got to go with John and David to beg orange crates from the neighborhood stores because I was a girl, and grocers would give to me easier than to a boy, so they said. I could also be ballast, giving weight to the orange crates being pulled home on our wagon. Daddy got involved with the second clubhouse, getting real lumber and tarpaper to cover it.

John and I parted ways in the teen years. For one thing he did not have the ability to comprehend very deeply, so I just stopped sharing at some point. I know that I was often embarrassed by him, but more often by how others treated him. John coped by moving away from those who jeered, and he won approval by getting good-natured laughter with bright shirts, various cowboy hats, and bolo ties. When I went to Sacred Heart Academy in Cullman for my last two years of high school, John went to Tuscaloosa High. We both graduated in 1960. Then we both moved—John out of state with our parents and me to Cullman to enter the monastery.

John went to trade school and learned carpentry skills. Daddy often worked with him to help build his skills. Then John worked as a carpenter in Virginia, often in high-rise apartments as they were being built. But jobs came and went for him. Finally, he was hired by LogEtronics as a mechanical assembler, a job he held for almost twenty-seven years. His company made photographic equipment for glossy print magazines. John did the cabinet work on the outside of the machines.

John always lived with our parents. He could not drive, but he knew the public transportation system extremely well in the Washington, D.C., area, taking several buses to and from work each day. In 1983 when our parents retired to Benedictine Manor in Cullman, John moved into his own efficiency apartment in Southern Towers, the same building where he had lived for nearly twenty years. He thrived in his work, his church, and with a large circle of friends.

Everything came to a dramatic end for him in October 1998. It was an intense family experience—heart-rending, awesome, yet deeply joyful. John kept telling his story during that month with all the details. I will try to do the same here.

John had been feeling bad for several months, but the doctors found only an infection. By Monday morning, September 28, he was very weak and unable to breathe when he walked over the interstate to the grocery store. Someone called 911 and he landed in ICU at Alexandria Memorial Hospital. For four days doctors tried to decide if he had TB, pneumonia, congestive heart failure, or something else. John called Mother in Cullman Wednesday night, after his friends finally got through security and into his apartment to locate his phone book. John remembered *every* fact he *ever* learned, but he had never learned Mother's or my phone numbers because he never called us. He thought a long distance phone call cost him too much. Mother always called him each week.

All the next day I was on the phone trying to get in contact with the doctor to learn what was happening. By the afternoon I learned that lab tests were finally in and indicated cancer cells in the fluid taken from around his lungs, obviously in an advanced stage. I asked the doctor not to tell John the diagnosis until I got there. I flew up on Friday in trepidation, thinking I would be the one to tell John that he had cancer. Mother was unable to go because of her weakened heart.

I found John sitting in the hospital bed, perfectly calm, praying his evening prayers. In a sibling judgment I thought, "Oh, no! He already knows the diagnosis, and he is trying to get holy really quick." I found out that one of his many doctors had given him the news earlier that day. Very matter-of-factly John was announcing to each person that entered his room that he had "the C word." In a few minutes Father Charles Merkle III from Blessed Sacrament (John's church for thirty years) arrived, got the news and went right to work with confession, anointing, and Holy Communion—a man of action just like John. Only then did I look at John's prayer books. He had leather-tooled covers for his two daily prayer books, and they were both *very* well worn. He told me RENEW did the best thing for him by teaching him a form of daily morning and evening prayer. Could it be that my brother was already holy!

Our sister Rose arrived from San Diego on Sunday. What a great blessing that the three of us together could experience the great drama that unfolded in the following days. Rose and I liked John's style of asking all hospital personnel as they entered his room what their rank was, what they were going to do and why. Then he could repeat in detail, a la John style, all they told him. He made his needs known immediately, but never whined, complained, or asked for special attention. We remember him saying: "It's backing up!" (about his pee) "It's making noise." (about his nose when he did not get enough oxygen) "Take it out!" (about the fluid in his belly)

John's passing was a three week drama. Each day brought new information and different decisions to make. In the first week he had to face the reality of "the C word," a word he feared since our Dad's death of liver cancer in 1984. But now that it was his turn, he accepted all matter of factly. One morning in the second week, it took only an hour's conversation for John to face the fact that this cancer was in an advanced stage. We told him he could not live alone any longer since he would have to go through needed therapy. I suggested that he come with me to Alabama. That meant he would have to leave his whole life in Virginia. But I suggested we could have a party before the move in order to say good-bye to all his friends. Immediately, John was on the phone calling his friends to arrange the party, setting the date for October 18.

But then in the third week, as deterioration continued, we knew John could not make the trip to Alabama. He then had to make the hard choice of chemotherapy or hospice. I asked him if he knew what hospice was. "Yes," he said, "Nice to know you."

He spent a full day processing that decision. His wonderful friend Edna, a co-worker at LogE for twenty-six years, came after work to help him decide. The next day, October 14, the morning of his 59th birthday, John told the oncologist he chose hospice, in his simple straightforward fashion: "Why drag it out if you are going to die anyway?" The doctor sputtered, totally confused about how to convince his patient of what he considered a needed therapy. John could cut directly to the essence. For him life had a simplicity, but that did not mean it was easy. Rose and I were impressed that he did not feel sorry for himself. What was, was. After making a decision John got on with the business of living and did that fully.

The rest of that day, John's birthday, was a wonderful celebration—full of phone calls from co-workers at LogE, visits from faithful friends from his church or his club (Prime Time Single Catholics), a day of balloons, cakes, and flowers. John's circle of friends was great. Bob Scudo and Gene DeAngelis, who had had Friday supper together for decades with John. Edna Toney who took his pet Rusty Bunny and visited so often. Celeste who gave John a stuffed bunny just like Rusty. Al Royston and three other LogE vice-presidents. Jim McNeil who lived in John's apartment building and often drove him places. Trudy and Verl Gibson, Mother's friends, who visited daily. All the Prime Time club members, especially the president, Katherine Speck, who kept adjusting the party plans as John's condition changed. All the priests from Blessed Sacrament, who each in turn visited. The sisters from St. Rita's. The list goes on and on.

The day after his birthday, although fully conscious, John was unusually quiet, just wanting us to sit beside him and hold his hand. The disease was advancing. I now look back on those days and think of him like a sheep being led to the slaughter. He knew he was dying. He wanted to die well. For John that meant not to complain, not to curse God, to go willingly, to surrender into God's arms. He did this quietly, though he was in a lot of distress as the various body systems malfunctioned. As I held his hand, I began to have a great pain in one spot on my back. I had a sense that the cord that had always linked us rather closely was now being severed. It was my time to let go too.

On the 16th John was moved to Woodbine Nursing Home and entered the hospice program. He died that night in his sleep, at 1:10 a.m. on Saturday the 17th.

The Good-Bye Party had been scheduled for Sunday, October 18. Rose and I, not to be outdone by John's decisiveness, called for the party to go on. At 7:00 that evening we had the Wake in the chapel at Blessed Sacrament. All sixty seats were filled and then some. Afterwards we went down the hall to have the party that John had planned. John was a great collector, wood-worker and leather craftsman. He loved cute and clever things. The walls of his efficiency apartment were covered with these collections. We took his rack of bolo string ties to the party. Many of these were decorated by John with leather tooling or wood carvings. Each person took one and wore it. Then after an excellent spread of luscious food we told stories and remembered John's life. I heard a lot about his love of dancing that night. I learned even more about what wonderful friends he had.

The funeral was on October 20. Many of the attendees wore John's bolo ties. He was buried at Fairfax Memorial Park, with his stuffed bunny under his arm and wearing his owl tie slide. (Oh yeah, he loved owls too—wood, ceramic, metal, plastic, leather, large and small. We stuffed five Xerox boxes full for the church white elephant sale.) Afterwards a dozen friends lingered over lunch.

I would be remiss not to also mention my gratitude to the Sisters from St. Rita's Parish, Fran, Terry, Karl Ann, and Therese. When I arrived in Alexandria they took me in on the second day after a brief phone call, without knowing who I really was. Rose and I stayed with them for a whole month as John's drama unfolded. They offered us quiet and restful nights after intense days.

John had lived many years in a very large city, in a large highrise apartment building along the main interstate highway into Washington, D.C. He could easily have been lost in the crowd. But not John. He always stood out. He related to everyone.

He could have been a target of unscrupulous people. Our parents had always worried that someone would take advantage of John when they were not there to protect him. They had tried their best to prepare him for an independent life. As I walked through his world that month, I learned that all the angel people of the world were responding to his zest for life and were looking after him. Alexandria, Virginia, is a mixture of people from all over the world.

His apartment building had a majority of Middle Easterners. Everyone knew him.

At his branch bank in the next building, I stepped up to the teller and asked if she knew John McGehee. *All* the tellers turned and looked at me and nodded. The loan officer said that John was always one bright spot in an otherwise very dull world of the bank. The manager walked me to the door and said how much she admired John because he always knew to the penny what was in his checking account. "That was my parents' hard work," I said.

When we thought John would be moving to Alabama I went to his grocery store to see if I could get boxes for packing a few things. John told me to look for the "heavy set black lady." I found Clem and she was helpful. The next week I returned to tell Clem that John had died. She gave a great laugh, slapped her thighs and said loudly, "God is in for it now! God is going to have his hands full with John." I knew that she knew my brother well.

I can too easily take my family members for granted. They have always been there. It was not until I witnessed this great drama of John's end of life that I could truly stand in awe of the wondrous gift he was to me and to so many people who were struck by John's total presence to the moment, his uniqueness of character, his zest for life. I have a deep gratitude to God for the beautiful gift of John's life. I am thankful that his suffering was relatively short, and that he is now home.

REFLECTION

Take an interior step back and ponder each of your own family members.
What is a unique gift within each one?

What does this reflect about our God who created these unique individuals?

Chapter 15: **PASSAGE THROUGH DEATH**

Mother always walked with a bounce in her step, full of energy, but contained, rational. She taught for seven years before she married. Some of those years she taught in a one-room schoolhouse on the Kansas prairie, riding a pacer there and back home. She was ever a teacher throughout her life. She survived the Depression and the Dust Bowl days as a young adult in Kansas. She loved gardening and walks in nature, always giving the scientific and the common name of each plant, tree, and bird. She wore the latest fashions, sewing her own clothes with seams better than in any store. Hair was always just so. She was an expert tour guide of the Washington, D.C. area, loving the history of the place in her eighteen years there. Though she was disparaging of women's lib, she was definitely an independent woman.

In 1983 my parents moved to Benedictine Manor in Cullman. Daddy died after a short illness of liver cancer a year later. Mother's passing was a ten-year process. When Mother was eighty-four I saw the first sign. She had lost her sense of good judgment and started giving her money away. This woman who had cooked every meal we ever ate, sewed each item of clothing we ever wore, pinched every penny we ever had, was giving her money to any telemarketer who called. I was horrified. I tried reasoning, but that was useless. She was upset that I was upset. It was a very emotional transition for me as I realized I had to be the parent and needed to take care of my mother who was the child. Once I had that straightened out within myself, we found a way to work things out. Mother gave me financial power of attorney. She had always been the one to handle the family money, so it was a very hard transition for her. Almost every day she appeared at my door with a handful of bills to be paid! I merely dumped all the begging letters in the wastebasket after she left.

It was that same year that Mother began getting lost when she drove in Cullman. Her sisters in Kansas convinced her to stop driving. She came home from the trip there and sold her car the next week. A real stripping for her, a loss of her independence, but she quickly learned to use CARTS to get around town.

Even in Mother's deteriorating mental state she was a beautiful example to me. She went to daily Mass and prayed for an hour each morning and each afternoon during all of her retirement years. She suffered with an arthritic hip that caused increasing pain. Mother's daily prayer had always been the rosary. With the added pain in her hip she changed to the Stations of the Cross. In her last year at Benedictine Manor she used her walker to stand on that aching hip so she could be close to each image on the wall of Jesus' path to Calvary. She told me she united her pain with Christ's pain and for the needs of all those in our world who suffer in any way. There was no self-pity or masochism involved. Mother was a mystic in union with the suffering cosmic Christ. Her prayer had to have had cosmic effect.

Then she had to deal with the physical condition of congestive heart failure. Mother's strong will and beautiful spirit kept her busy with gardening and the exercise program at Benedictine Manor. But gradually with the physical deterioration, the mental processes were affected even more. First, there was short-term memory loss, then growing dementia. At age 93 Mother needed to go to an assisted living facility. I heard her say repeatedly, "I don't know why Mary stuck me here." But I also had a twenty-year-old memory. Before moving to Cullman, she had asked if they would infringe upon my life in coming south. She did not want to be a burden on me. In her first year in Cullman, she looked all over town for a nursing home so I would not have to do that task when needed. Those memories ameliorated the later words of complaint.

The last two years of Mother's life were very weighty for me. Ever in the teacher mode, I wondered if she were teaching me more of life's lessons. I resisted. Enough was enough! I continued my ministry of retreat work and spiritual direction, as well as coordinating Contemplative Outreach Birmingham and carrying responsibilities within the community. But I had many added responsibilities with Mother's care. I had to train the staff to respond to Mother's needs and check on them, make doctor visits, check medications, and hire and monitor sitters and hospice workers. I had been teaching prayer for years, especially the practice of mindfulness. As all this drama unfolded, I was getting *the* lesson of my life about living in the present moment. And every moment was different, unpredictable. Phone calls in the night, unexpected things happening in the day. I was really strung out!

On Thanksgiving Day there was an added tragedy. Aunt Mary and her roommate Melba were in a terrible auto accident in Kansas City. Since only my cousin Frank lived near them, and he ran a farm, I went to help. I stayed three weeks, until Aunt Mary was discharged from the hospital and settled back at home, returning to Cullman less than a week before Christmas. Each day after that Mother lost some functioning, until her death a week after New Year's. The time was a whirlwind.

On New Year's Day there was one moment of pure gift to me. Mother had rallied some on that day, although mostly I saw the demented old woman lying in her bed. Yet there was one instant when I looked at Mother and saw her old self, the Mother I knew. I could see very clearly how utterly tired and filled with pain she was. With her true-self eyes, she looked at me and said, "I love you. Thank you for everything you are doing." I was deeply moved, and received this last gift.

The day of Mother's dying was another kind of wonder. By that time Mother was unable to respond, and simply lay in bed breathing in a more and more stressful manner. The sitters had been putting in twelve-hour shifts for days, so I had given them the entire day off. Sisters volunteered to do anything needed, so Sisters

Maurus, Bertha, and Regina took several hours each. I was on my way there after lunch when the hospice nurse came in and found Mother in the dying process. Sister Veronica and several others came. Father Kevin arrived to offer the Last Rites. Maurus, Priscilla, and I stayed. We prayed, sang, told stories, ate supper, watched and waited all day and into the night.

Susie Baldwin, a Yoga student who was dealing with breast cancer, came and sat holding Mother's hand. I felt as if the Old Woman was saying to the Younger, "This is all part of it. Living and dying is all gift. When your time comes to go, it will be okay. God is waiting. Life is good."

I sat at Mother's feet and held them. At first when I held them I felt lots of jittery energy. It seemed like all the indignity she had been through in the recent weeks—all the strangers changing her diaper, bathing and turning her, handling her old body. Gradually that jerky energy subsided, and I felt the strong pulse of life, utterly visceral. My whole body resonated with this pulse. As the hours passed, we continued praying, waiting, being with Mother. The breathing and the heart beat changed. Death came easily, with the releasing of the last big breath. And all was quiet. The pulse of energy had gradually passed. It was as if I were standing at the edge of the next world, holding her toes as she stepped into the Kingdom. I could almost see into the Mystery. I stood in awe.

Later after I finally got to bed I awakened several times, and I could still feel my body resonating with that great pulse of Mother's life. I wondered at the image of her closing scene. She, who had given me birth from between her legs, was now born into fullness of Life as I waited at that same place.

A month after Mother's passing I was talking with Glenda, one of Mother's sitters. She said, "I have your mother's picture on my mirror. Every morning she talks to me."

"What does she say," I asked.

Glenda responded, "She says: 'Well. What interesting things shall we do today?'"

Yes, that was Mother's spirit. Even in her oldest, most tottering state, she stayed upbeat. She sought life. No self-pity or whining. No paranoia or blame. Always drawn toward life and beauty and things that lifted the spirit.

******

In the year after Mother's passing, there were many more deaths around me. Aunt Catherine, Mother's youngest sister, died some months before. My good friend and Yoga teacher for thirty years, Priscilla Lovoy, died after a two-year battle with colon cancer. Priscilla's life hallmark was to live mindfully, to see the beauty in each person and in all of life and to celebrate it. Deacon Al Girodo, administrator of Corpus Christi Church in Oneonta, died in a quick two months with a brain tumor. Al and I had served on the Peace and Justice Commission together. His was always a strong voice and pen for justice in our church and our world. I miss his fiery words and fierce heart. I visited these dear friends numerous times during their illnesses and led their memorial services.

In my monastery eighteen of our Sisters died within a six-year period, from 1998 through 2003. Some who died had very significant meaning to my life journey: Sisters Raphael and Monica in 1998, Sister Barbara in 1999, Sisters Mary Susan and Martina in 2002.

I was totally worn out. I asked for and received time for sabbatical in Ireland. I had the wonderful fortune to spend a whole month in Glendalough, a beautiful valley of two lakes surrounded by mountains. My hope was to rest, to sleep as late as possible, to walk slowly in nature, and to be kind to myself. But what did I find? All that had happened in the past several years of care for Mother came back to me, but especially my harsh words, impatient gestures, and irritated responses that had jumped out of my mouth in my frenetic state. No, I did not find Mother correcting me or blaming me. She took no offense. She would remind me in a very simple manner, "Well, you don't have to use profanity." But there in Glendalough I was haranguing myself for every shortcoming that revealed itself in the past two years.

The evening of my sixth day on retreat I sat outside my hermitage eating my main meal while Father Michael Rodgers, the retreat director, was working in the garden. I asked if I could talk with him. He responded, "You are supposed to be a hermit. Stay in the garden." So I muttered away as I went back into my house, lots of internal commentary going on, "Doesn't he know who is asking for help? I never ask anyone for help. Mutter...mutter..." On some level I knew it was the old desert father saying, "Go to your cell, and your cell will teach you everything." I just did not want to hear that at the time. I wanted a little human response.

That night I had what I needed in a dream, and everything changed for me. The long dream was just like an ordinary day in my life. It went through all the details of working with a retreat group. One of the participants was in some kind of crisis. Betty Giardini, a counselor friend, was helping me with her. Mother was on my right arm (as she so often was) tottering along with me. Suddenly Mother collapsed onto the floor. I ended up beneath her, holding her.

The dream was exactly like my waking life, yet there was more weariness in the awake situation—phone calls at all hours of the night and day with her mother-voice on my answering machine whipping me into shape, the human dynamics of the staff caring for her, ups and down of her physical condition with doctor visits, medical worsening (often after a change in medication), getting each situation set up for her ever shifting state of health, changing as her health deteriorated, driving back and forth each day, buying supplies, etc., etc. My, how voiding and urinating are such big deals! Beside her care, I knew I had other things to do each day—teach the Psalms or Yoga, give a massage or listen to a sad story or a boring one as a spiritual director, give a retreat or plan a program, take off down the road to give a retreat or program elsewhere, attend a meeting. And be civil to everyone. Aaack!*?!

As I awoke from the dream, I realized the closing scene of the dream was like the *Pieta*. It felt very strong to me and I lingered in its vision. That is what I had been doing all along—holding the body of Christ, holding my suffering and dying Mother. I stayed in awe a long time, absorbing the scene, not even needing to forgive myself. The interior haranguing was ended. I was absorbed into the Mystery.

When I saw the *Pieta* in my dream I did not analyze it, I just sat with it. It seemed to touch some deep part of me. I communed on soul level. In the Pieta I realized I had not just carried a load a long time, enduring Mother (which is sometimes how I felt) but loving her deeply, whole body, whole psyche—to the cross and beyond.

Later upon reflection I realized it represented the big picture—what I had been doing for the last ten years, holding the crucified one. I had spent an untold amount of energy trying to make things better. But really there was no way to make Mother better, only one step after another of deterioration, body and mind failing bit by bit. My frustration and impatience was *my* agenda to "fix things," to improve the situation. It all definitely needed monitoring. No one should be left today alone in a hospital or nursing facility without an advocate, a protector. But the best that any person can really do is to hold the bleeding, dying crucified one. There is no way to make it better. This is the Mystery of God…not mystery as puzzle or the hunt for an answer. But the Mysterion…the wonder-filled work of God birth, life, death, Life. I later learned the word *Pieta* is Latin for "loyalty and devotion."

I sit in awe and wonder,
Holding the body of my strong Mother, my feeble dying Mother,
Time of metamorphosis,
of the shedding of all that is walking, breathing life,
of surrender into another realm,
of letting go.

Easter images,
of shedding the cocoon,
leaving the caterpillar worm existence behind,
flying free.
Breaking through the egg shell of old knowings,
hatching into unbelievable Life.
All the Passover images.

But hard, so hard, Passion of Christ hard.

Used up entirely.
totally consumed,
burned brightly by God's love into other form,
incense burned,
deep *YES* into Mystery.

All is okay, held and cared for
by Mother love into Life.

  As my time in Glendalough went on, each of my dear
friends and Sisters who had passed were very strong presences. I
wept for each of them. There were new little lambs in the April
fields. I found myself baaing with them as I walked the valley and
mountains. I was utterly lonely, abandoned by so many significant
people.

Then one night I had another dream. It was a dream of one scene only. I was standing beside one of the lakes at Glendalough. Standing just behind me to my right was "my brother" (not John) tall and strong holding me as I leaned back against him. I woke up with the very visceral sensation of being held. I knew I was not alone. What gift. I lingered with the sensation and the knowing.

In the following days my disposition changed to one of deep gratitude and thanksgiving for the presence and power of each beautiful person in my life. How was I so fortunate to have so many very unique, very ordinary, and very wonderful people in my life? I walked in celebration and in praise.

One day upon climbing the highest mountain in the area, I found a cairn of stones on top. I returned there on one of my last days to leave stones of remembrance for Mother, Priscilla, and Al. Each of them spoke to me. They all told me I had mourned enough, and that it was time to return to the marketplace.

Mother, the interrogator: "What are you going to do next? When will you start? Where will you do it?"

Al Girodo, with gravelly voice: "Mary, get on with it! Do something about this war in Iraq. Do some peace creating."

Priscilla, with utter sweetness: "Whatever you do, I know it will be wonderful! It will be beautiful."

I am ever grateful that my faith teaches me of the Communion of Saints. I can no longer see these dear friends and family members in the flesh, but I still feel their presence. I know their love and encouragement. I count on it,

REFLECTION
Who do you mourn?

What shape does your grieving take?

Do you experience the self-critic?

Is there any possibility of forgiving yourself?

Chapter 16: PUT YOUR SWORD AWAY

It is Advent, December 17, the day on which for centuries the Church has sung the great O Antiphon—O Wisdom, O Sapientia, O Sophia! This is the feminine principle that has inspired all creative works, the God-birthing force of all life and order.

It is more than three years since September 11, 2001. As that fateful day was revealed hour by hour before all of us on our TVs, my first thought was that the attack could be coming from any continent because the United States has messed with people's lives all over the earth. People in every part of the world have reason to hate us. My next thought was that the United States in turn would be going to war and cause thousands more to die, be maimed, and made refugees. The horror before us was terrible enough, but it would fuel even greater horror. I wept for all the victims. I wept for my refugee daughters who mistakenly thought that at last they were safe and freed from violence.

In the following months I pondered the images of 9/11. Why were those targets selected? I well could have missed discussion about this question, but I never heard or saw an attempt at explanation. Yet it seemed quite clear to me. The World Trade Towers, those lovely pinnacles reaching to the heavens, represented U.S. economic domination. We have taken the best natural resources and goods from every country of the earth for our own use. We have justified ourselves by saying that worldwide we are giving people jobs, not admitting that we do not really offer a fair trade, and that we definitely give a substandard wage. The Pentagon represented our unlimited military might. We have sold arms for profit, *for profit*, to every armed conflict globally for decades, and we have used them ourselves. We have amassed thousands of weapons of mass destruction. We have nuclear bombs set to go off on hair trigger alert. We strut that we are the one and only

Super Power. We have forgotten the old story of the Tower of Babel. We think we are Gods, and that we can do anything we want.

My friend Jerry Levin, who was a hostage in Lebanon years ago, called 9/11 the first sacking of Rome. He said that "Rome" has already lost her soul. I have to agree with that comparison.

I ponder that on 9/11 the talk was immediately of terrorism and of our retaliation. I had just watched the perpetrators immolate themselves in the planes that exploded. The word "terrorist" did not fit. They were not just trying to make us afraid. They were saying something utterly more desperate. This was some other category. How could we get a grip on the level of despair before us? How can one retaliate against the already dead? In the United States since then we have moved into war with Iraq motivated by our own great fear. Iraq was the nation we bombed in 1991. Then for twelve years we held economic sanctions against them and continued weekly bombings, not allowing them to rebuild. Now we were bombing repeatedly a second time. We asked why those people did not love us for ridding them of Saddam Hussein, a man who previously was our collaborator for years. We have continued our old illusion of military and moral superiority, wanting to exterminate the evildoers, whoever we decided they were, with whatever means we chose to use. We did all of this justified with Christian slogans.

I weep for the soul of our nation and our world. I remember Jesus' parting words to his best friends at the end of their last important evening together, "Put your sword away. All who live by the sword will die by the sword." When will the violence stop? Will we ever hear the message of nonviolent love and reconciliation offered by Christ Jesus? I celebrate Jesus' resurrection message that he gave over and over, "Peace! Shalom! Do not be afraid!" His is not a mamby-pamby peace, but courageous peacemaking and truth speaking. Jesus knew well the might of the super-power of his day, Rome. He chose not violent resistance, but love.

I look within myself and see the violence, anger, and rage I have been acknowledging and wish to release, but that has such a firm grip on my soul. I realize I am unable to clean up my own act. I am a mess. I pray with today's liturgy:

"O Wisdom, O Holy Word of God
you govern all creation
with your strong yet tender care,
Come and show your people the way to salvation."
Vespers Antiphon

Yet when I get really still I also acknowledge that God is doing it. God is loving me and all my sisters and brothers of the earth, despite our brokenness and hardness and ugliness. God looks at all the darling creatures on the earth and pours out in love. I ask that I may become an instrument of that Love. Oh, that I may be Christed, that there be less and less of me and more and more of the One of Total Love. Do it. Take me and transform me as You will.

With this desire I wish that the rest of my life be used up in peacemaking and bridge-building among people—within my own heart, within my community, within my nation and my world. Such a desire is really scary. What will it call forth from me? I know it means sharing my own pain and suffering and vulnerability. I know it means I must continue my daily earnest prayer, lest I forget Who really is in charge. I know it means at least twice a year I must have deep stops of uninterrupted time and silent space in a hermitage somewhere with nature to ground me. The rest is up to God.

I am left with a further challenge given me this Advent during a retreat by John Dear, S.J. John pointed us to various Gospel passages to ponder Jesus' nonviolent way of loving. There were two passages about joy that particularly caught my attention. First was the Magnificat of Mary, that prayer that I have prayed every evening for more than forty-five years. That young unwed Jewish woman living in an occupied territory could boldly proclaim God's saving acts. In a seemingly hopeless situation while under absolute

116

control by Roman military might, violence, and superiority, that peasant woman could enthusiastically rejoice and utter prophetically:

"The Mighty One has done great things for me...
God has shown the strength of his arm,
and has scattered the arrogant of mind and heart.
God has thrown down the rulers from their thrones
and lifted up the lowly.
The hungry God has filled with good things,
the rich, sent away empty..."   Luke 1:46f

May I have such seeing, such faith, such boldness, such joy in my God.

In the second passage John the Baptist, Jesus' friend and cousin, is speaking just before his execution by King Herod. He, who seemingly should be terrified, speaks a message of awareness and deep joy:

"The bridegroom's friend who stands there and listens
is glad when he hears the bridegroom's voice.
This same joy I feel, and now it is complete.
He must grow greater
I must grow smaller..."   John 3:29-30

I ask for this mystical knowing, this wonder of standing before the Bridegroom and being full of joy with the knowing. I ask for the eyes to see the Fullness already at hand. We do not need angry peacemakers. We need ones full of joy because they are filled with God's presence and love. May my heart be so filled.

I often like to imagine armies of peacemakers, trained with nonviolent conflict resolution, who will stand boldly and lovingly before those of the world who wish bloodshed. I hope that such peacemakers will work together for reconciliation and understanding of all peoples of the earth. We have shining examples of this multiple times within the last century—with Gandhi before the British Empire in India, with the Civil Rights movement in the South, with the people of the Philippines who ended the Marcos regime, with blacks of South Africa ending apartheid, with Solidarity in Poland, etc., etc.

May this love force that sees all of humankind as brothers and sisters grow stronger and stronger. May we all rejoice in God our Savior who is called by many names.

REFLECTION
Take a few deep breaths…
Calm yourself…
Imagine a lovely meadow of green grass
waving in the spring breeze…

See peoples of various nations dressed in their folk costumes coming from different directions, singing traditional folk songs in their native languages.
Feel the energy of each kind of music.

They form a circle of human connectedness.
The circle spirals in dance, gracefully intertwining,
Dipping and turning, hands joined of all peoples of the earth.
Each person is necessary, no one is left out.

They dance into the Light.

Chapter 17: MY HEART REJOICES

As I look back over my life with its cycles and seasons, I realize that about every ten years I have had significant time on an extended retreat. Those extended retreat pauses have felt like a pouring out of myself before God, a rooting deeper into the Mystery, a grounding into the one thing necessary—to be in God. Each time God has then taken me and shifted and changed things in some remarkable ways that I could never have predicted: from Miss Perfect to monastic seeker, from disillusioned monk to refugee mother and social activist, from Amazon warrior for justice to survivor of breast cancer, from survivor to witness and healer of many wounded souls.

I do not know what lies ahead, but I remember and revel in God's gifts of life and love. I know that God's inbreaking is total gift, that I only have glimpses of it at unexpected moments—in the crystal covered frozen forests of New York, in my own backyard facing a refugee, through healings on the massage table. Those moments of deep seeing help me to know the reality I walk in daily, one shot through with God's gracious love and beauty. My prayer is that I may continue *to see*, to really see the Mystery right before my eyes. My hope is that despite my own hardness or confusion I may *receive*, truly receive the gracious gifts with which God blesses me, and that my heart may become filled with *gratitude*. My heart rejoices in God my Savior!

This dream arrived the morning after Christmas:

I am walking in a mountain pass. A large white bird and several baby birds emerge from a aloft in the rocks on my left. The large bird is a snowy owl. She flies up and off to the right, her wingspan enormous, glistening white, wonder-full. I am awed by her sheer size and her beauty. She leaves four tiny white fluffy babies behind.

I turn to look back at the babies and see two huge black birds among them. I am struck by the black and the white. All were feeding on something. When the two black birds lift their heads, I realize they are buzzards.

As I awaken I am horrified that the buzzards may be eating the babies. But then I realize I am seeing the fluffy babies moving, alive. All are eating something in their midst that I cannot see. The dark birds of death and decay with the glistening children of the great snowy owl.

Acknowledgements

There are so many I wish to thank for their part in my writing of this spiritual autobiography. First and last, I must thank the God of Love for forming me and drawing me ever more fully into the Divine Mystery. David Frenette was especially instrumental in helping me listen deeply one day, a listening and an inspiration that gave shape to the writing that came later. If it had not been for the Sabbath Leave Program offered by Samford University in Birmingham during the fall of 2004, these reflections would never have been put on paper. Because of the grant from the Resource Center for Pastoral Excellence these ponderings have come into printed form. I especially want to thank the staff, Kristen Curtis and Molly McAllister, for their daily office support while I was at Samford.

I must also thank Dr. Fisher Humphreys and Sister Maurus Allen for reading my manuscript and offering their words of wisdom. Fisher was most encouraging to make the leap to have the reflections published.

It was the time in stillness that provided the needed inner space to put my reflections on paper. I thank Sisters Jane Connor and Geraldine Whelan for their encouragement while I stayed at their hermitage at Blessed Trinity Shrine Retreat for two weeks in October 2004. I thank Dr. Wendy Arthur for the use of her cabin Solitude during my final week in Advent.

My thanks go to Sister Veronica Ryan, my Prioress, and my other Benedictine Sisters for all of their encouragement to take eight months of sabbatical rest and delight. Because they continued working, I was able to be freed. I especially thank Sisters Bridgid Clarke, Jane Bishop, and Karen Ann Lortscher for taking me into their home for the fall months when I was at Samford.

Since this writing my teacher and mentor and very dear

friend, Maurus, has left this earth suddenly on Ash Wednesday to soar into the arms of the Beloved. I miss you, Maurus, and send you a lifetime of thanks.

My heart rejoices in God my Savior! My gratitude cannot be expressed fully enough.